KAT KERR
Foreword by Scribe Angels

REVEALING HEAVEN

AN EYEWITNESS ACCOUNT

ILLUSTRATED BY
WALTER REYNOLDS

One unique thing about this book, is that the Lord asked me to get the endorsements from everyday people, like you and me.

Kat Kerr's book, *Revealing Heaven*, is an exciting, beautiful account of Heaven. God has allowed her to bring us into the most mysterious place in the universe so that we may know His greatness and purpose for us in Heaven while we are still earthbound. My favorite part of the book is about the amusement park and now I know when I get to Heaven, I can ride roller coasters. The chapter about the babies in Heaven brought me the most peace because I have two children there. It's a book of promise, transformation, truth, and joy! It is a holy book and Kat Kerr has blessed the nations with this precious revelation. Many of us have dreamt of such things, and kept them in our hearts. No one will read this book and remain the same!

___Monica Schroyer Wife, Mother & Youth Leader

I was overwhelmed by what I read in **Revealing Heaven,** the Foreword captivated me and made me consider my own life. Ms. Kerr did a great job. It was fantastic and everyone should read it!

__Henry 'Hank' Foncenot
Security Guard, The Woods Development

AMAZING!!! Really Amazing! I laughed and cried with joy! Kat's obedience to the Lord in writing *Revealing Heaven* gave me fresh hope and the desire to walk with Him now and live with Him then, forever and ever. **I am still in awe!**

__Judy Owens
Hair Specialist, Strands

I believe that this book will bring great comfort to those who have lost "saved relatives or friends", and cause those others to search out the things of God through Jesus Christ to ensure their inclusion in Heaven and not Hell at their passing. This book helps to give a better mental picture of what is waiting on the *other side* after our short pilgrimage down here. I have always had a great fascination with books written by people who have had visions of, or visitations in Heaven. ***Revealing Heaven*** with its wonderful illustrations adds an element that was lacking in the other books. It is Incredible!

__James Hyde
Husband and Mentor to children

Revealing Heaven brings an eternal perspective to everyday life and takes the mystery out of the supernatural. Kathy Kerr's divine encounters bridge the gap between the physical and spiritual realm. Each story reveals a compassionate Father who understands the importance of connecting His family for eternity. This is a book to share with everyone who has lost a loved one. It will help families understand an eternal connection and bring hope during time of loss!

__Susan Dyer
Elementary Principal, Providence School

Do I believe all this or not? That's probably what you are going to think to yourself when you read this book. But hey, why wouldn't Heaven be everything and more? God said everything is possible through Him, so of course everything in Heaven is possible. I know all about this book and at times I thought to myself, this lady is crazy; but God has blessed Ms. Kat, definitely! The things she saw is so beyond my imagination and let me tell you, I have a big one. I know the Lord will speak to you as you read this book and broaden your vision of Eternity!

__Glori Lee

Teenager, Dance Student

I was pleasantly surprised as I read this book that many of the questions I've had about the death experience and the afterlife were being answered. This book brings hope and deepens our understanding of God's overwhelming love for us, which dispels the fear of death. It is truly wonderful to know that our Heavenly Father has prepared such a beautiful place for us to live with Him for all eternity!

__John Rumbach

Husband, Purchasing Agent

NOTE FROM THE AUTHOR

You choose where you will spend Eternity – no one else! Through this book, the Father is offering you a 'glimpse' into eternity by showing you some of the things He has prepared for His people in Heaven.

To ensure this book revealed His purpose, I was assigned two scribe angels to assist me in separating the book into the different chapters. They also delivered (at the instruction of Holy Spirit), the 'Foreword' for this book. It is a prophetic proclamation from the Father about His 'Glory" which is about to cover the whole earth. This proclamation contains both warnings and promises that will be fulfilled when it happens. It so powerfully affected me, that it was several months before I could print it. It is a HOLY word for this season of God we are entering into. Everyone should take it seriously, especially those who are leaders in the Body of Christ (the Church)!

I was somewhat concerned when the Lord gave me instructions for the book to be illustrated, because I can only do 'basic' sketches. What a relief when He said Walter Reynolds, a prophetic artist, would take my sketches, receive revelation from Heaven and give me a beautiful finished product. All of the illustrations were the combined effort of Walter and myself.

Although beautiful and true in content, I did not include everything that was present at the time I sketched them. I felt that there are some things that should remain 'covered' until you see them yourselves. Especially, the scene of the Throne Room where there were many details I left out; the cherubim who support either side of the throne, the seven lamp stands, the four living creatures, the elders and their thrones.

It would have been humanly impossible to capture all the Glory and perfection that is Heaven; however, He has allowed this glimpse to give you HOPE! Because of His great love for humanity, He has allowed me to share the experiences I had in that holy, beautiful realm. It is the single greatest assignment He has given me and I pray it changes the lives of millions of people so that Heaven becomes a reality and no longer a myth.

The wing on the cover of the book is a representation of the four Living Creatures, who stand guard at the four corners of God's throne. They are covered with eyes in front, in back and under their wings. You may read about them in Revelation Chapter 4. I have seen the wing of this living creature appear many times over the congregation in our church, usually during worship. Their eyes are ever seeing!

If you are wondering about my 'pink hair' on the back cover of the book, it was not my idea. It sounds wild, but God actually asked me to put the pink highlights in my hair (it was very humbling). He wanted everyone to know that He would accept them, no matter what color of hair or skin they had.

Please take the time to read the Foreword and Introduction which come before the body of the book and then be sure you see the Author's Bio and contact information at the back of the book. A lot of prayer and consideration was poured into this whole work!

God is about to do something that will forever change this planet and the people on it. *He is bringing Heaven to Earth!*

Kat Kerr

FOREWORD

(A prophetic Proclamation from God)

By

The Scribe Angels

To Him who sits upon the throne, we give Praise, Honor and Glory forever and ever, that He would desire to reveal His home in the Heavens to the men of the Earth. **Rejoice, O Earth, Rejoice!** For Heaven is about to kiss you and when it does, the Fire of His Passion will consume every living being. He will forever leave His mark on the hearts of millions and they shall come to know Him as their Savior. Be thankful citizens of Earth that you are living in this day and hour, when the Glory of the Lord will cover the whole Earth. How magnificent in His ways, how mighty in His acts is the hand of Him who sits upon the throne. In eternity they shall sing about these days – the great and powerful days before the end comes. All things will be shaken and all things will be restored to and through God's faithful believers!

Prepare O enemies of the Most High, to be made His footstool! None will escape His Glory and there will be no place to hide from His Light! He who has chosen this handmaiden to reveal the hidden things, the precious things, and the treasures stored up in His Heaven for those who love Him and love the coming of Him! We, His faithful Scribes, created by Him in the beginning to serve in His celestial realm and to record the words of those we are sent for; and to deliver and release His messages to those whom He trusts–are grateful to be a part of His divine plan in revealing Heaven.

Prepare you faithful ones, whom have stood under much warfare and devastation of the enemy. Prepare to receive great reward, now, in this lifetime and in the glorious life to come. You are about to see the power of your God released, and you will truly know that He is in control.

Behold, His fire comes to blaze across this world and into the hearts of men, to push back the great darkness and claim His creation back to Himself.

Prepare men and women of God, those who watch over the souls of their congregations–to yield to Holy Spirit of God when asked to lay down your plans, man's plans, and allow Him to take control during this hour. For those who yield, there shall be great increase of anointing in your ministry. For those who refuse to yield, your place shall be given to another and some will even sleep early!

Prepare your hearts, for He must first visit His leaders and then His church body. **Will you all be able to stand and carry this Glory, or will you be exposed by its coming?**

The bowls before the altar are tipping and the veil of flesh has been torn; nothing or no one can stop what is about to happen! Manifestations of His power through signs, wonders and the miraculous will happen everywhere – no buildings will be able to contain them. **He will no longer be put in a box, nor will He wear any man's tag,** but He will unite His true Body of believers and the World will know them by their love for each other! Prepare to hear a new sound – the sound of Heaven!

This is a glimpse into Eternity! Prepare to read. Prepare to be forever changed. Prepare people of Earth, for starting in the year 2007, God is *REVEALING HEAVEN!*

AMEN! AMEN! AMEN!

Cherubim's Wing

INTRODUCTION

To use mere mortal words to describe the 'Glory' of Heaven is not an easy task but, since I have been persuaded by my Lord, I will attempt to do so!

God has a 'time line' throughout eternity and he has chosen this appointed time to reveal what He has prepared for those who love him and have accepted His son, Jesus, as their Savior. I am continually overwhelmed by the grace and goodness of God for allowing me to visit His celestial realm for over 10 years. Even though I never asked to go to Heaven, He chose to take me for His purposes.

The experiences mentioned in this book are not about me, nor were they for me. Never, during any of my visits did I know that one day I would write a book. That assignment came when Jesus appeared in my home and commissioned me to write about His home.

Over several years, I was shown many fantastic places and things. During many of my trips to Heaven I was taken to the houses of the Redeemed who wanted to let their families know how God had blessed them. Sometimes I was shown children who had passed away and the relatives they were living with in Heaven. No children are ever left on their own.

I had never met most of these people, nor did I know anything about them. At no time did I ever speak directly to them, but I was allowed to observe and hear their conversations. Upon returning to earth I was able to share with their loved ones what I had observed, which caused Heaven to become very real. It brought great hope and many times dispelled grief knowing that their loved ones were more alive in Heaven than they ever were on earth! You do not cease to exist, but it is like 'moving' to the most fantastic place where everything you desired is already waiting for you.

Sometimes I visited places that were created solely for fun and entertainment. Believe me, Heaven is not boring! If you think you have to give up 'things' when you go to heaven, you are quite mistaken.

What makes *Revealing Heaven* a little different from other books that have been written about Heaven is that it contains 'evidence' that what I saw, actually exists there. You will see this in the chapter titled "Dearly Departed".

The most overwhelming thing I can share about Heaven is being in the presence of Jesus. When He casts His gaze upon you everything fades away and you are consumed by His Glory. As He approaches, hosts of angels go before Him declaring His holiness and you are engulfed by the radiance of His beauty. Standing there, perfect peace washes over you, wave after wave of love flows through your entire being, and you become 'undone' as Isaiah did (see Isaiah 6).

I have seen Jesus several times before going to heaven and He has even spoken to me, but each time I am moved by the experience of being in His glory! My prayer is that you, too, will someday stand in His presence!

This book is not another 'study' on Heaven, but simply a story about the things God allowed me to see during my many visits. It will not only transport you to His realm, but through the illustrations, you will actually view many of the things I saw while in Heaven. God gifted me to sketch the places you will see and then connected me with a prophetic artist, Walter Reynolds, who brought them wonderfully to life!

Please know that it is not my job to convince anyone that the things revealed truly exist; that is the job of my best friend, Holy Spirit, whom I love dearly. This knowledge completely frees me to not only proceed with the assignment given to me by God, but to thoroughly enjoy doing it.

Most of these trips were never forewarned to me, nor were they made according to my timing. I was just 'taken' at the will of Holy Spirit. Each event I share will have a small intro as to any special circumstances that were occurring when I was taken.

If you were to ask how I qualified to become an ambassador for Heaven, it would not include a long list of 'religious' credentials.

Instead I would have to tell you that I love being a servant to God's people. It was instilled in me by my father, from the time I was a child.

My family (I am one of 15 children, 4 are now in Heaven), although not wealthy, has always reached out to help the rejected, the poor and the forgotten. Many mornings I would wake up to find people sleeping on our floor, because my father would go out at night and bring in the homeless. He would take our food, sometimes right off the stove (which didn't always sit well with my mother), and give it to others who had nothing. My Papa truly had God's heart for those who were suffering; and my mother learned how to be an intercessor and pray in more supplies. Now, many years later, at age 54, I love helping people and have taught my three daughters to do the same.

We were also taught to be faithful and to serve at the church God had joined us to. We did not just worship and fellowship there, we gave of ourselves and tithed too. I love my church, New Life Christian Fellowship, where I have been a member for over seventeen years. Our pastor and his wife (actually, their whole precious family is involved at the church) love people too. Our motto there is, "Worship God and Celebrate people".

That is why when asked to help in Hospitality, my mother and I said, "Yes". That means for almost six years we volunteered to decorate, prepare meals, serve them and clean up. This took place at some regular weekly meetings and several special events. Some of my trips to Heaven are related to a few of these events. Others happened from my home, parked in my car, walking outside and even while shopping. I have lost count, but am always overwhelmed each time I am taken.

There is NO other place like Heaven. No matter how you try, your imagination and creativity could not come close to that of the Father. There are places that look similar to what is on earth, but some of the supernatural stuff will blow your mortal minds! I am still trying to figure out some of it and being a 'simple' person doesn't make it any easier. I only know one thing, no one will want to miss going there and there is nothing on this planet that is worth losing the chance. If you are bound by any sin that would prevent you from going, please just repent and surrender it to Jesus (I John 1:9).

He will help you because He loves you! Nothing is impossible with Him, no matter how hopeless it appears to you. He created you, died for you and now lives for you. The bible says, "He died for us while we were yet sinners".

He will never leave you or disappoint you! Not only does He give you eternal life by accepting him as Savior, but He will empower you with His Holy Spirit to triumph in your every day life. Read the bible and find out what His blood has won for you. We will have trials while on this earth, but He is able to deliver you out of them all. He has already won the victory for us.

Many times, when I am still, the music, sights and aromas still come to me as if I had just left there. Also, sometimes when I am out walking, I can feel the 'wind of the Spirit' swirling around me and that same 'awe' comes over me that I feel when I am in Heaven. It is like getting *kisses* from above, reminding me that He cares and knows where I am. It is hard to live a normal life here on earth, when I know what is waiting in Heaven. It is probably a good thing they never asked me if I wanted to stay!

I want to let you know that I have been confronted with many trials over the years, but none to the degree I have faced this past year. Sometimes they were almost unbearable and even with my gift of faith, I wondered if I would survive the onslaught. But always, I would triumph with the help of God's word and the voice of Holy Spirit.

Although I had been to Heaven and had mysteries revealed to me, it did not negate me from facing the same attacks that are common to us all. I have learned that through it all He will keep you in perfect peace. So press in, worship Him, and declare His greatness and evil will flee as you become a 'sacrifice of praise' unto your God. The devil cannot bear to be where the presence of God dwells.

As you read, prepare to be amazed, overwhelmed and encouraged for what awaits those who choose to call Jesus their Savior and thus, Heaven their future home!

I give thanks to my heavenly Father, his son Jesus, and Holy Spirit who allowed me to see the Redeemed and their mansions in Heaven; also, to the two scribe angels assigned to assist me for this season of my life. May God give them the grace to put up living with a mortal and the patience to work with someone who many times gets lost on her own street!

**GLORY, HONOR AND PRAISE
TO MY HEAVENLY FATHER, MY LORD JESUS AND
HOLY SPIRIT
FOR EVER AND EVER!**

SPECIAL NOTE

Please check RevealingHeaven.com for Volume II and III which will be a continuation of my journeys to Heaven. We are also currently working on a children's series based on this book, authored by my younger sister, Jen. All books (including narrated versions) will be translated into most of the known languages, so that the nations can glorify God for His goodness. Please rest assured we are currently working on these translations and although we understand your hunger and urgency to see this happen, we will not give permission for translating or publishing to take place outside of our own publisher, Xulon Press. Those who willfully violate our copyright laws will be contacted by our legal department for appropriate action.

For inquiries see contact information at the back of this book.

TABLE OF CONTENTS

As it is written, Eye has not seen, nor ear heard, neither have entered into the heart of man, the things which God hath prepared for them that love Him. But God has revealed them unto us by His Spirit.
I Corinthians 2:9, 10a (KJV)

CHAPTER ONE

GOD'S DESIGN–EARTH IS A
SHADOW OF HEAVEN

I would like to begin by explaining what God told me, that earth is a shadow of Heaven. In other words, most of what is here on earth already exists in Heaven. It is not a flat place in the sky, floating around covered in clouds with fat baby angels dropping grapes into our mouths. It is a literal spiritual 'world'; round, just like earth, only huge in proportion (bigger than our Galaxy)! Hebrews 8:5 talks about things on earth being a shadow and type of what is in Heaven.

Many things here have always been there, only perfect! No death, decay, rust or pollution at all! Everything is beautiful–almost beyond description. God-inspired ideas eventually made it into the mind of man and were then invented here on earth. All 'good' things created came down from the Father (James 1:17). It is our enemy, satan, who has perverted and defiled things on this earth and he uses people to promote and desire these wicked things. There is neither evil nor its influence in Heaven. There are also many things in Heaven that have not yet been invented here. We only use a small percentage of our brain power, but in Heaven we will be unhindered and creativity will be fantastic.

There are places in Heaven where we will actually invent and learn to create. One of the places of education is called 'Creation Lab' which will be discussed in Volume II.

Earth and Heaven operate in two different realms. Our natural 'physical' eyes cannot see into the 'spirit' realm (unless God opens them); but the 'spirit' realm can see everything in our 'physical' world. This earth operates in a 'physical' realm because we have physical bodies. However, inside your body is a spirit body, which operates in Heaven (which is a 'spirit' realm) in the same manner as on earth.

You can touch, taste and smell things just like on earth, only in Heaven all of your senses are magnifed. It is actually hard to tell whether you are there in spirit or in your body because you do still have these senses and you experience emotions; you do not become a robot! When you die and go there, you do not become 'invisible', able to pass through things, nor do you turn into angels.

God's word in Hebrews 11:16 talks about Heaven being a city and a country, just like on earth. There is an awesome city where the river flows from under the throne and another area I saw had miles of countryside. Many of the people living up there refer to this as the 'park'. It is definitely different from the city I visited in Heaven. The park is where you can see every species of animal ever created; including the dinosaurs which roam the hills (they all eat grass, or at least it seemed to me they were eating it). There are beautiful meadows, hills, creeks, waterfalls, trees and the most glorious flowers you could ever imagine.

People living in Heaven have their own secret garden designed by Jesus. So, when they want to be alone with Him, they go in there and He comes.

The city, where the throne room and river of life are, is magnificent. Everything reflects the glory (light) of God which is why the 'streets of gold' are transparent, so they will reflect His light. I have only seen a small part of it, but there were people going into buildings and stores. Heaven has a lot of activity!

I saw different styles of transport vehicles, which all run on 'light' – it is the only source of fuel other than the wind that blows the sails in the big ships on the crystal sea. People travel across Heaven in many different ways–air transport, ground (yes, they still have chariots and some even come with hyper-drive) and on the sea in all types of vessels. Mostly, I saw individuals using 'public' transportation in groups, but I definitely saw individuals piloting or operating these vehicles by themselves too.

I have only briefly experienced 'thought' travel, where you just 'think' of going somewhere and you are suddenly there. It may not have been me at all, but rather accomplished through the angelic beings who escorted me. I did see people get onto a 'moving' path, so that is another way you move about in Heaven.

One of the best things about Heaven is that you do not need money to 'purchase' things; everything is free, because it is 'given' to you. Everyone has 'assignments' rather than jobs and they are always connected to their particular natural gift, which makes it a joy to do. That's why I saw restaurants, art galleries, sports arenas (sports are played as worship), movie theaters and even an amusement park because when you move to Heaven you will use that natural creative gift God put in you! You receive no 'payment' for your efforts as money would be useless there, since everything you need or want is given to you. In this way, all gifts and talents are used to benefit everyone!

Some of these places will be thoroughly discussed later in chapters of this book and others in Volume II or III. The interesting part is how I found out that these things and places existed. I was just as delighted and surprised as you will be to find out what God has created for all those who will live there.

It really makes sense that if we were made in God's image, the earth would be made in Heaven's image. There are, however, many 'supernatural' things and places there that will challenge our mortal brains. I was so overwhelmed that usually I did not think to ask, "What is that"? Both Holy Spirit and the angels told me that Heaven is always increasing and adding new things for our enjoyment! God wants to bless His people and one of the ways He expresses love is by creating things that will delight us. His word declares in Psalms 37:4, "Delight yourself in the Lord; and He will give you the desires of your heart".

No one will want to miss going to Heaven, and the alternative, Hell, (which will be discussed in chapter 9) is not to be desired by anyone!

God is the Great Creator and Heaven is His home, so why wouldn't it be exciting and fascinating to live there? I pray you will be encouraged to know where your loved ones are living and some of the places they are enjoying, so let the journey begin!

CHAPTER TWO

LIFE AFTER DEATH–
THE JOURNEY BEGINS

The Word of God says, "To be absent from the body is to be present with the Lord". This is a promise God gives to all Believers (those who have accepted Christ).

This chapter will explain what happens to someone from the second they die and their spirit leaves the body and earth can no longer hold them. First, we will discuss what happens to someone who has accepted Jesus as their Savior and will be going to Heaven. Then, we will discuss what happens to someone who rejected Christ and is headed for Hell!

Whatever has brought them to this moment, whether natural death at old age, a sickness or disease or an accident, it is always the same. As you draw your last breath and your spirit begins to leave your body, you will begin to feel weightless and float upward. If you look back, you will see your lifeless body. If there are other people in the room or area where your body is, you will also be able to see them and hear their comments. You cannot communicate with them, because you have left your 'physical' body and are now a 'spirit being' entering the spirit realm. Yes, you do still care about those you are leaving behind because you love them but you are now entering into the precious promise of God–to be with Him. Unfathomable love erases any anxiety or fear of death you may have experienced, even moments before.

If you were sick, injured or in pain before, you will now realize that all those symptoms have completely left and that you feel wonderful. Also, if you were elderly, you are now young again because age has no effect on your eternal spirit. The life of God now flows into your being. You will have no fear, because the peace of God will now become your constant companion. At this point, some people still do not realize they have even died; because they still have their senses and can touch themselves, it is hard for them to comprehend. They will still try to communicate with others that they pass by and wonder why they do not respond.

If not already present, the angels will appear to escort you on your journey to Heaven. They are magnificent beings still aglow from being in the heavenly realm. They always know your name and always assure you that all will be well. No one is left to find their own way. If it is a child or baby, they are carried by the angels; they never experience fear or sadness, only tremendous love. There is no 'hanging around' or a struggle to find a way to 'cross over'. No one's spirit can remain on the earth for very long. There are various ways to be taken to Heaven, including chariots. If Jesus comes to escort individuals, they get to go in the Lord's own chariot. It is rare, but sometimes loved ones are allowed to see you leave or to see the angelic beings who have come to escort you.

One of the normal ways you are taken to Heaven, if you are to remain there, is by a transport. These transports come in many different models, so they may not all look like the one I saw two years ago when I witnessed someone boarding one. Not only could I see the ship, but the two angels who were escorting the woman. She looked amazingly beautiful and young, even though I knew she had been very old when she passed away. This transport (as shown in the illustration) looked something like a cable car without the cables.

The lower part was made of a solid substance that looked like burnished pewter. Ornate panels, on either side of its doors, were gold as was the trim that ran down both ends of the ship and around the bottom. The light emanating from the sides as well as from beneath the ship was a brilliant white with blue highlights. This could be the 'bright light' mentioned by some who have had 'near death' experiences.

The upper part of the transport is like glass – you can actually see through it. Can you imagine how exhilarating it must be to streak through the universe and see everything on your way to Heaven?

You usually enter from the side of the craft by way of steps that appear from nowhere and have no visible means of support. How supernatural is that! I was told that sometimes people are also brought up through the bottom entrance (which I could not see).

Sometimes angels navigate these crafts, but usually people are chosen for this position before they die. They become Heaven's pilots, not because of prior flight experience, but because of their heart for people. They have a natural ability to put people at ease and to share things about the new home they are going to.

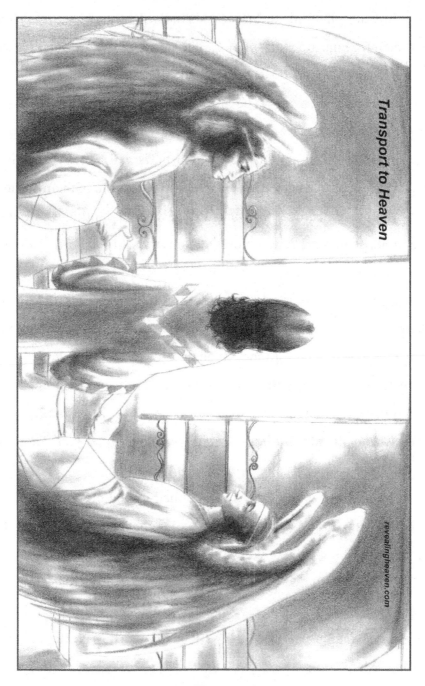

The Transport

Heaven's pilots are the first contact individuals have with Heaven and therefore must be trusted by God to portray His care and love. It is a high honor to be chosen for this assignment.

It was truly amazing to be able to see a transport close up. The angels who escort these transports all wear white gowns with purple sashes at the waist, and purple on their cuffs and hems. They also wear narrow purple bands on their heads. At least one of them carries a sword. Once boarded, the transport leaves and continues through the atmosphere at speeds we only dream of, until they arrive in the third heaven.

Once the transport stops, you will be escorted out and left in the care of other angels and / or people whose job it is to welcome you to Heaven. Many times Abraham will be there to greet you. Sometimes the gates will be visible from your disembarking point, but sometimes they can be some distance away. Your family and friends who already dwell in Heaven will run to greet you. There is much joy and celebrating going on at your arrival.

All this time you will be overwhelmed by the presence of God and the beauty of just being there and experiencing the sights, sounds and aromas. You feel like you have truly come home. Just when you think it can't get any better, Jesus comes! You are now taken into the throne room where the redeemed and angels worship and rejoice together. Worship can be singing, dancing and bowing before the throne. Many times Jesus will dance with His people; everyone wants to touch him. There are times of celebrating and times to lay prostrate before the King of Kings. On the way to the throne, you are greeted by all those whom you pass by. As you approach the throne the brilliance of the Father begins to overwhelm you.

The Living Creatures proclaim His holiness (Revelation 4). You can hardly bear to look upon the glory of the Father as He declares His love for you. Fire and lightening proceed from His presence and awe falls over the throne room. Everyone turns to watch as you are welcomed home.

Just when you think you will collapse from the weight of the glory, God reaches out and holds you to Himself. Never have you experienced such love and acceptance! All your preconceived ideas as to what God is like are washed away in the flood of love that goes right through you. It is unconditional love and you finally know the passion that was in His heart when He sent His Son to the cross for you! You are truly complete!

Next you are taken by your family to your mansion which has been lovingly prepared for you. Everything you ever desired in architecture, style or décor has been considered to please you. Even the landscaping of your property is suited to your taste.

If you had any pets on earth that were special to you, they are also waiting for you (recreated by a loving Father).

This is the time to enjoy your welcome home party. And then, you are taken on an extensive tour of Heaven by your family and/ or friends. You visit all the wonderful places your loving Father has prepared for you to enjoy. He truly delights to give you pleasure.

Now, we will describe what happens to someone who dies without accepting Christ as their Savior. At first, they will experience the same exact sensations as the first person, but that begins to change almost immediately. They too, will no longer be sick, crippled or aged. As stated before, everyone's spirit is eternal and once you leave your physical body (no matter what condition it is in) you will have a perfectly made spirit.

You soon begin to feel the sinister presence which is coming for you and then suddenly, demons appear and take hold of you with their claw-like hands. Horror fills you as the stench of death fills the room. You are unable to fight back, because Satan now owns you! No matter how you fight or scream no one will come to help you. Your family and/or friends cannot see nor hear you and even if they could, they would be helpless to prevent what is about to happen. When you reject Christ, you become the property of Hell when you die. They begin to pull you downward until everything disappears into darkness. You begin to feel the heat and hear the screaming and moaning of agonized souls.

Even though your spirit was whole when you left your body, it will not remain that way for long. Hell is also a spirit realm and because you are now a spirit being, you will feel every form of torture they have. As you enter into the yawning mouth of the underworld, other demons will start to yell in glee as they begin to mutilate your being. The pain and agony is real and fear rules supreme as your mind begins to realize what has happened to you. All this time the searing heat is blistering you and every horror you ever thought has become real!

There will be no contact with another human being (I never saw people together there), other than the sounds of screaming and cursing made by those sentenced to everlasting punishment. You will never eat or drink again, although you will experience continual starvation and dehydration. Never again will you know rest or peace, just utter exhaustion and pure terror. Your mind will reach the brink of insanity, but never allowed to completely go there. There is NO escape. You are there because of the choice you made, not because God rejected you. You will remain in Hell until the end of the millennial reign of Christ upon the earth. Then Hell will give up the wicked dead and they will go before the Great White Throne Judgment where they will receive their eternal place of punishment (called the second death) which is the Lake of Fire. God is merciful, but sin cannot enter into His presence nor dwell in Heaven because He is HOLY. If you do not receive Christ as your savior, your name will not be found in the Book of Life and you will be thrown into the lake of fire. Be sure you know where your destiny lies before you die; because after death it will be too late! Also, NEVER stop praying for your loved ones salvation while they are alive, it may be the only hope of divine intervention to persuade them (even while in a coma) to seek Christ. Do you know where your eternal place will be?

CHAPTER THREE

THE ANGELIC HOSTS –
REAL PERSONALITIES

This is one of my favorite subjects, because the angels are so real to me. I have seen many angels over the years and the variety never ceases to amaze me. I would caution you, however, to remember that satan can take the shape of an 'angel of light' as described in 2 Corinthians 11:14. It would not be a wise thing to 'call' angels to yourself, as this could be used by the enemy to deceive you. All of the angels I have had contact with were sent by the Father. I never initiated or requested that they appear or come to me!

Many of the angels I saw were very strong and muscular, especially warrior and guardian angels. Warrior angels are very powerfully skilled and fiercely determined to carry out their tasks against any enemy. They are defenders and protectors, able to stand up to any demonic being. They take their assignments VERY seriously.

Angels do not operate like robots, although committed and unswerving in their dedication and love for the Father, Son and Holy Ghost, they do have emotions, feelings and opinions about us! We are actually a mystery to most of them; wondering why we do the things we do and sometimes act as though God does not even exist.

Some angels that are assigned to earth at this time have a height of nine feet and some as large as twenty feet. There are extremely powerful angels who are reserved for the end times (as mentioned in the book of Revelation) and their size is immeasurable.

God does assign angels to the earth, as stated in Hebrews 1:14, to care "for those who will inherit salvation". Some of the most unusual are the Guardian angels who are assigned to you from conception. Their main task is to protect and guard you from harm and to report to Heaven concerning your spiritual growth. When we are making good progress they are elated, but if we do just the opposite, it frustrates them.

Angelic beings can and do change their appearance like that of a human (Daniel 10:16) and have many times been among us without our knowledge. Since they are 'spirit' beings and not physical, they can also appear and disappear. Always, their greatest desire is to please the Lord at all times and because He cares about us, they will use every power allotted to them to fulfill their assignments.

In Heaven, one of the order of angelic beings is the seraphim, who actually have fire coming out of them. They operate in close proximity to the throne and therefore reflect and carry God's glory. The book of Isaiah, chapters 5 and 6, reveal this heavenly being and how God used them to purify the lips of the prophet with coals of fire. There are also the 'living creatures' that are covered with eyes, even under their wings (Revelation 4:6). They stand at the four corners of the throne and continually proclaim the holiness of God!

Angels very often receive training for special events or movements God has planned for the earth and right now there is tremendous angelic activity here on the earth. As stated in the 'Foreword', God is about to do a tremendous work here!

CHAPTER FOUR

DEARLY DEPARTED – LIVING IN THE CELESTIAL CITY

Almost everyone has at one time experienced grief over the loss of a loved one. It overwhelms you and leaves a big void in your life. You cannot replace them no matter how we sometimes try. Only Jesus can heal and fill that place. The one thing that helps is knowing that they are in Heaven and we will one day see them again. I hope that the following stories will encourage you to know – HEAVEN IS REAL. When you go there your life does not stop – IT BEGINS! If those there could come back they would tell you – "I am home". Please believe that God has kept His Word – we will live because Christ lives!

This is one of the most exciting chapters in this book as you will learn about actual people who have passed on, what they are doing and how this knowledge impacted the lives of their families when it was shared with them. Permission was obtained from each of the families involved.

All of these trips I took to Heaven were done under different circumstances and I will relate each story exactly as it happened. I have made other trips and seen other people in Heaven, but I will save them for Volume II. At this time, we will focus on three different events.

Maurissa – A Destiny made in Heaven

This particular event took place in February of 2001 and even though I had been to Heaven many times, this trip will always hold a special place in my heart. It shows the unfathomable mercy of God and how much He cares about us! I will start by explaining the circumstances surrounding this event. My Mother and I had just completed setting up and serving for hospitality at a four day conference held at our church and we were very tired. The following day we received a call from the church asking for a favor from the pastor's wife. She wanted to know if we would clean a woman's house (named Esther) who had just hosted out-of-town relatives for several days for a funeral. My Mother received the call and even though we were exhausted, she said we would grant the request.

We had heard that a young person had recently died as a result of a skiing accident, but knew nothing else. She did not attend our church, nor was the funeral held there. Apparently, this woman, Esther, was related to that young person. I will now share what happened while cleaning Esther's house.

We arrived around 2:00 p.m. and I started dusting. After being in the house for just a few minutes, Holy Spirit and the Lord started talking to me. **This is what was said, "You know, her Great Grandfather met her at the 'gate' when she arrived. I asked him whom he was talking about and He said, "The young girl who just passed away, the granddaughter of Esther. I want you to tell her mother, Melodee, this message because she is grieving for her. Maurissa is now living with her Great Grandfather because, of course, she is too young to live on her own. He is showing her the time of her life and is taking her somewhere to have lots of fun."**

(A split second later I was in Heaven)

I heard this high, excited laugh, and then I saw her. She had shoulder-length, reddish-blonde hair and was grinning very big. I was not certain of her age, possibly the early teens. She was holding the hand of a young man with reddish-brown hair (even though he was her Great Grandfather, you do not remain old when you go to Heaven). He appeared to be in his mid-twenties and quite pleased about their coming adventure. Maurissa, filled with joy, seemed barely able to control herself, knowing where he was taking her. She was also with another young person, a girl, several years older than she was and she had straight, long blonde hair. It was not revealed to me who this third person was, but Maurissa was very happy that she was with them. I saw all of them walking down a beautiful wide pathway. The flowers were breathtaking, every color you could imagine and every petal was perfect. I had never seen anything like them before.

Amazement rushed over me as I realized I was approaching an amusement park. There were very tall trees on both sides of the path and in the distance I could see a huge roller coaster. You could hear the people screaming with laughter as the cars on the roller coaster plummeted down what looked like over a several 100-foot drop. (The Holy Spirit later told me the name of that particular coaster was "The Rush").

(Just as quickly as I was taken, I returned to earth.)

The Amusement Park

Still standing in front of the fireplace mantle, the **Holy Spirit said, "Maurissa is a joy to be with. Everyone liked her and she was full of life and energy. She always had a positive attitude and was a blessing to her mother and her friends. They all miss her very much. Please tell her mother that she is now her greatest cheerleader and will cheer her on to the destiny I have planned for her".**

He then let me hear these words that had previously been spoken by her mother, "I can't believe she is gone. Her life is over and she never got to fulfill her destiny. What will I do without her? I want to know that she is okay. I want her to know I love her!"

Then the Lord said (for Melodee), "Your daughter chose to stay because she knew her greatest contributions would be in Heaven. Please tell everyone that I did not take your daughter, but I knew she would be here early and that her destiny would be made in Heaven. She is now a leader of the youth (age does not matter here, I judge by a person's heart) and is in charge of organizing the youths' contribution to the celebration in the Marriage Supper of the Lamb. It is a high honor for her, but I know she will do a super job. She will not overlook a single detail and will include all the youth so everyone will have a good time and none will be left out. Your daughter has a very BIG heart. Why would I choose anyone else for this assignment? She has embraced the task and is going forward with it, and as usual, giving a 100 % of herself. She loves you dearly and knows that

you feel the same about her; but she would ask that you release her now so that she can fulfill her destiny.

She said when she sees you again one day she will kiss you on both cheeks and tell you everything that has happened to her here and will make sure she leaves nothing out. She always enjoyed talking with you and being with her friends.

She was everyone's friend and is the same way here. Your personality does not change when you come to Heaven; it just blossoms and becomes even more pronounced.

Maurissa dwells in My presence now and I will make sure she is taken care of and not left on her own. I can give you grace to help if you ask Me. I can heal the hurt, if you let Me. I will never take away her memory because she is too precious to you, but you can walk in My peace and I will release it to you right now. Trust Me. Seek Me, for I desire to draw closer to you and tell you of My love for you. Don't ever be afraid to say anything to Me; your words are important and I will always take time to hear you. You too have a destiny to complete and now you have a faithful cheerleader here to root you on to fulfill it. I will send other children to you that will desperately need to be loved. Don't refuse them, for your love will make a major difference in their lives and destinies. It may be the only Me they ever see. I love you, My daughter".

After I experienced all of this, I called my mother from the other room and told her what had happened. I then called the church to let someone know what I had heard and they gave me the telephone number for Maurissa's mother, Melodee. I made arrangements to meet her and give her the message. After typing it all down, I drove to a local mall and met with her. While reading the message to her, she turned white and looked quite shocked. Following is what she shared with me when I finished giving her the message.

Laughing and crying at the same time she said, "There is no possible way you could have known. No way at all! I have never met you and you were not at the funeral service. When I asked her what she meant, she said, "I know that everything you told me is true and I know you saw my daughter in Heaven. I know this, because the day I returned home from the ski resort I was looking through her room and I found something. It was a journal my daughter had kept back in 1995 (she was 13 years old at her death in 2001). As I sat reading, God led me to a journal entry dated October 3, 1995, where she had written about a dream she had the night before. It said she dreamed she died early and went to Heaven early and that she met her Great Grandfather, and went on a roller coaster ride."

Journal,   10-3-95

Once I dreamed... that
Jesus took me up to heaven
early. And I got to see my
great grandfather early.
I got to hide all kinds
of rollar coasters. I
did see tons of machines.
It was wonderful. But
when Jesus took me
up he only gave me a
peek so as fast as
rollar coaster I fell
down. Bye Bye.

Maurissa's Journal Page

After telling me this, she continued to tell me about her daughter Maurissa. She was exactly as I described her –slim, strawberry blonde hair and that she had actually been a cheerleader at her school. She also told me that Maurissa was very popular and had always desired to be a leader when she grew up. She had impacted so many lives that they bused students from two different schools to her funeral. Hundreds came and many made decisions for Christ.

Maurissa was a very special young lady! I continued to talk with Melodee and shared some of the other things I knew about heaven. Then I prayed for her and went back home. I was very blessed to know God had used me to help Melodee through a very difficult time.

Statement from Melodee Nobles, Maurissa's Mother

March 13, 2007

To Whom It May Concern:

After losing my only child, Maurissa, in 2001, I found myself searching for answers. I was trying to find peace and comfort in the midst of my darkest hour. I was going through what I call the "pit" of grief. I literally would have done anything to see my child again. I needed to touch her, feel her, smell her, anything to gratify my loss of her physical body. The ripping away of her flesh was most apparent at this time. There were days I told my husband, it may sound morbid, but I miss her so much, I just want to dig her up and just hold her! I would go in her bedroom, lay on her bed and just scream and cry into the pillow.

A short time after Maurissa's death, my mother called me to tell me an intercessor at the church had received a vision of the Lord for me in regards to Maurissa and her untimely death. My initial reaction was one of skepticism. I was raised in a Pastor's home and began to question whether this was actually from God or possibly someone trying to get "in" with the pastor's family.

I met with Kat after work one night just outside of J.C. Penney's and immediately felt God's comforting presence as she walked over to me. She said she wanted to give the message to me in person. Contained in this message were little "kisses from heaven" that Maurissa and God the Father sent to me through the comfort of the Holy Spirit. She said things in this message that only Maurissa would have known. Kat did not know me, my family or my daughter. When Maurissa was little, I would have her kiss me on both cheeks before dropping her off at school. In her message Kat wrote "and when I see you again Mommy, I will kiss you on both cheeks." Another heavenly kiss was that when Kat typed her message from the Lord to me, she was told to print it in blue ink. That was Maurissa's favorite color, her cheerleading color, the color of her room and everything we had done for her celebration service was in blue ink. One other significant kiss was that there was no possible way she could have known about the 'dream'

Maurissa had written in her journal in October 1995. She wrote that she had died early, met her Great Grandfather in Heaven and went on a roller coaster ride. These were similar to the very words Kat started her message with, an undeniable proof that Kat was hearing from Heaven!

Death is not God's plan; His plan is for us to have eternal life and life more abundantly. It is not His desire, nor does He punish us by allowing our loved ones to be separated from us. He will send you "kisses from heaven." Kat's message began a road to recovery for me. I am now able to live with this loss and continue God's plan for my life, so that my daughter's destiny can be and will be fulfilled. Since Kat's first message, I have had dreams and visions of my daughter, Maurissa, and it has opened my eyes to a spiritual world where there is total joy! Kat and I have had many conversations about heaven and when I tell her things, on many occasions she is already aware of what has been revealed to me.

I am also writing a book about this time in my life. I will share how God has shown me how to tap into His peace...the one that passes all understanding. I encourage you to tap into God. There is a thin veil between this earth and heaven. Our loved ones are more alive than we are here on this earth and one day it will be revealed to those who believe. I cannot imagine going through this without the hope of seeing Maurissa again. She was my whole world next to Christ and I have completely changed my view of eternity since this experience. Truly we are to be so heavenly minded that we can do earthly good.

Melodee Nobles (Maurissa's Mother)

Statement from Esther Zink, Maurissa's Grandmother

March 17, 2007

TO WHOM IT MAY CONCERN:

Kat Kerr came into our home during a crisis moment, the death of our 13-year old granddaughter, Maurissa Dawn Martin. We have not gotten over the emotion of it during the last seven years since her Homegoing to Heaven. Three Grief Share classes later, reading and viewing every book, video, DVD on death and dying, receiving many encouraging phone calls, cards and prayers from our family and friends (Body of Christ) we are resting in HIS PEACE!

Our Pastor's wife called the Kerrs to see if they would be willing to clean our home as a blessing. It was Kat Kerr's Mom who answered the telephone call and told Sharon they would be glad to help.

While Kat and her Mom were cleaning our house the Friday after the funeral, God spoke to Kat about Maurissa and her Great

Grandfather, who was already in Heaven awaiting her arrival. God even told her their names and other details that only God could have revealed to her. As she was dusting the fireplace mantel, God suddenly took her to Heaven and she saw Maurissa and her Great Grandfather going down a path to an amusement park. She knew Maurissa had strawberry blonde hair and was wearing blue and white. Soon Kat shared this experience with us verbally and in writing.

Two later visions Kat shared with us became even more detailed about what Maurissa was doing in Heaven. The burgundy and gold flowers, the lullaby music, the verbal messages were just a few of the outstanding details that let us know Kat was for real and only God could have given her this detailed knowledge about our granddaughter. Also, knowing she had never met Maurissa made her messages from Heaven to us even more miraculous! We desperately needed to hear her words. Each vision God allowed her to share with us was undoubtedly from the throne room of Heaven.

We had never met Kat before. She was a complete stranger to us; but each time she lifted us up into heavenly places as we read her visions from Maurissa in Heaven. If I had ever doubted visions from Heaven, now I am a true believer. Kat Kerr has now made me want to write about my near-death experiences. She truly does hear from God in Heaven because I have been blessed by her to receive inspiration, healing and victory. We can hardly wait to see Maurissa and all our loved ones who have gone home before us.

Kat does much more for God than anyone I know. She feeds the hungry, houses the homeless, has volunteered for years to cook and clean up for church gatherings and is truly one of the most hospitable Servants of Christ that I have known in my 66 years of life on earth.. Without her God-allowed messages from Maurissa in Heaven to our daughter, we would not be as far along in the grief process as we are today.

Melodee's Mom and Maurissa's Biological Grandmother, Esther Laurel (Owens) Zink

THE VALENTINE

It was Monday, February 14, 2005, and my mother and I were at the church preparing a breakfast for the monthly International mentoring meeting. I was decorating the tables and picked up some of the long stem red roses we had purchased to make a centerpiece, when I heard the **Lord say, "I want you to give some of the roses to Vickie and tell her they are from her husband for Valentine's Day. He misses her and wants her to know that he still loves her very much".**

I immediately turned to go down the hallway (I knew Vickie worked in the church office) and suddenly the heavens opened and I saw Jesus playing golf with John, Vickie's late husband. I was astounded and could hardly believe my eyes. "There is golf in

Heaven?" I asked, but they did not answer me. Jesus and John both had tunic tops and loose pants on (I mention in an upcoming chapter that you do not wear your gowns and robes all the time, usually only to corporate gatherings and in the throne room). *I realized that I was no longer at the church, but was now in Heaven.*

The course they were playing on was very beautiful; every blade of grass and every leaf on every tree was perfect. I don't know how the game was going, but they were certainly enjoying themselves. It was an 18-hole course, complete with a '19th Hole' club for fellowship after the game.

I stood there staring when **Jesus said, "This is John's backyard, his own private golf course, something he really desired. Come and I will show you his front yard".** I was really in for a shock, because the next thing I knew I was standing on a very royal looking deck overlooking the water (there is a crystal sea which comes from the throne room and runs all over Heaven). I do not know what substance it was made of, but it was very firm, like decorative concrete. It had wonderful intricate patterns over its large surface.

People were arriving by boats to visit and play on John's golf course. The boats, in an array of colors, made no sound nor put forth any odors because they were propelled by light. It was a delightful scene as John came over to welcome his guests.

There were beautiful awnings coming out from his home to form a magnificent entrance way. It appeared to be a type of 'Greek' design, as were the furnishings inside the huge home. It was very masculine and yet inviting at the same time. A lot of care had been taken to pick only the best for this home. You really do get your heart's desire.

John came in and I heard him say to some of the guests, "I wish Vickie could see this, it would really bless her. But what I really wish she could see is her own home; it is much grander than mine and she deserves it!"

Just as quickly, I was back at the church, still walking towards the office to leave the roses for Vickie. I could hardly wait to tell her what I had seen.

When I arrived, Vickie was on a break so I left the flowers with a detailed note. She called me later and with tears in her voice, she told me how badly her husband had wanted to play golf but could never afford it. God was so gracious to prepare the wonderful surprise for her husband when he went to Heaven and then to let Vickie know about it. It did bless her very much and it made it even more special, as I believe this was her first Valentine's Day without him.

Statement from Vickie D'Elia, March 26, 2007:

"For the first few minutes after you told me about the vision you had of my husband, John (or Johnny as I called him) I meditated on it. I thought to myself, if you had told me you saw him playing pool or bowling it would have been an instant recognition of him since he played both well. Then I realized by the Spirit that he had always wanted to play golf. In his latter years, he always watched the golf tournaments on television, read articles about it and even got a part-time job with a golf supply company. Johnny had become very knowledgeable about the game. He said, "One of these days I am going to take golf lessons", but financially we could not afford it and therefore never realized that dream before he died.

I cried after you shared with me about Heaven, because I realized Johnny had been given a desire of his heart. He not only was playing golf, but even had his own golf course. How wonderful God is to allow me to know about the gifts he gave Johnny and about the beautiful home he now resides in.

The gift of roses which were left for me were an 'instant' recognition of Johnny, because whenever he bought flowers for me they were always long stem 'American Beauties'. Instead of a dozen he would get me eleven, because he said I was the *12th American Beauty*! It completely overwhelmed me to receive those roses at that particular time, because not only was it Valentine's Day, but because the one year anniversary of my husband's passing was February the 12th.

God knew how significant it would be for me to hear from Heaven and know that I was still loved and not forgotten. It has helped me realize that life does not cease to exist when we leave here; it is just the beginning of the rest of our life"!

ON SAFARI IN HEAVEN

Message for Patricia Sweeting concerning her husband, Gerald Sweeting, who went to Heaven on August 12, 2005.

I was busy doing some research when we received a call from our church to see if we would do a funeral luncheon for someone who had been in prison ministry for several years. We agreed and they proceeded to give us the date, time and number of expected guests. That evening as we prepared to make our lists for the luncheon Holy Spirit began to speak to me. **"You must wear African style dress and take your mother's safari animal statuary to decorate with".**

This was something new He had not asked before. "Why," I asked? **"Because, he loves wild animals and it will bless his family. Also, I want you to get those gold jaguar shoes out of your closet and give them to his wife. Tell her that they will be a reminder of what I have given him".** I had almost forgotten about those shoes. I had an impression to purchase them several years before, but had never worn them. They were black and gold with a wedge style heel and on the side of each shoe was a five-inch long gold jaguar. Although they were very rich looking, they weren't really my style so I put them back in the box and shelved them. As silly as it sounds, I actually wondered if they would fit her. Holy Spirit assured me they would.

As soon as I stepped towards my closet, **I was instantly transported to Heaven**. I was not startled as I had gotten used to these 'instant' trips some time ago. I knew immediately I was outside the heavenly residence of Mr. Sweeting. An angel escorted me up the beautiful entrance drive which was lined on both sides with tropical plants, flowers and huge royal palm trees. The two-story home was magnificently made, each story being about 20 feet high. There were balconies along the second story so you could come out and enjoy the view of his property. As I was walking, I noticed that just a few yards away lay a lion and some cubs. They were playing in grass that looked like it had been imported from Africa. As a matter of fact, all of the grounds surrounding his home looked like what you would expect to see if you were on a safari! I could see and hear other animals in the area. How strange, I thought.

Upon entering the house I was immediately struck by the majesty of the entrance hall. Black ebony pedestal tables with gold (I am sure it was real) edging and designs. The walls had beautiful murals painted on them – all African style scenes. The sconce lights on the walls filled the room with a golden glow and enhanced every scene as I passed down the hall. Off this hall were several smaller rooms, probably used for personal 'private' meditation, prayer or just relaxing with small groups of visitors. All of them had leopard or zebra style prints on the upholstered furniture. One thing that stood out was the gorgeous, deep purple color used on accessories such as, throw pillows, floor pillows, runners or draperies at the tall windows.

The most striking room I passed was round and in the center of the room was one of the beautiful ebony tables. In the center of the table were two large decorative pillows which held two brilliant crowns, every facet of every jewel was perfect. They were different styles and I knew immediately that one was a 'soul winners' crown which Christ promised everyone who reached the unsaved and won them for the Kingdom of God. How they shone, it lit up the whole room and how exciting to know one day I would also have one.

At the end of the hall I saw Mr. Sweeting (even though I had never met him, I knew instantly who he was) talking to a young gentleman with blonde hair. I could hear lively music and laughter coming from the large room at the end of the hall. It was his homecoming party, which everyone receives when they first arrive. I heard the gentleman call Mr. Sweeting "Chief". Immediately the angel escorting me said, "That is the name which the Father calls him.

It defines who he is in the eyes of the Lord. Mr. Sweeting's robe looked just like something a wealthy African chief would wear. He was laughing now and seemed very excited.

He could neither see nor hear me, however, I was allowed to hear his conversation. He was saying how he wished he had been able to tell Patricia good-bye and that he was sorry he had left so suddenly. He also wanted her to know he had heard everything she said to him while he lay motionless in the hospital. He wished she could see what God had blessed him with and that he would continue to pray for his family back on Earth. I returned shortly after that conversation and proceeded with plans for the luncheon.

The next day we decorated for the luncheon as directed by the Holy Spirit. We used my mother's beautiful jungle animal statuary, candles, black and gold as accent colors, a leopard print table runner and African style greenery together with some small palms. To serve the meal, we used the sterling silver servers, crystal platters, china plates and satin tablecloths. The room's appearance was very regal.

Once the funeral service was over, the guests began to arrive. Everyone seemed to be impressed and when Patricia arrived, she looked stunned. She sought me out and asked how we had known to decorate with that particular style, as her husband loved it. I took her aside from the other guests so I could speak privately. I began by asking her why he liked the 'jungle animal' theme so much. I told her I thought maybe he collected things from Africa or he was rediscovering his 'roots'. What she said next stunned me!

With tears in her eyes, she said, "All his life he wanted to take an African safari, but I would never go. I was afraid I would be eaten by the wild animals so every time he asked me, I said no".

I proceeded to tell her how God took me to heaven and how he had shown me her husband's home that was built in the middle of a wild animal preserve. I shared about the beauty of his mansion and what I heard him saying about her. She was quite overwhelmed by it all, but was very moved at the goodness of God. She loved the gift of the jaguar shoes and, of course, they fit her perfectly. Her life was changed forever.

Patricia Sweeting's personal statement:

"I was so shocked when I walked into the funeral luncheon and saw how it had been decorated. I said, "Who did this? I want to know who did this". I was directed over to you and asked, "How did you know? Why did you use the African décor"? You then explained about how God took you to heaven and showed you my husband and all the things about his home there. I knew what you were saying was true even though you had never met me or my husband, Gerald.

The part that really got me was when you said he lived in a mansion on an African preserve; that you saw him dressed in 'royal' robes and God called him "Chief". What you did not know was that my husband had fallen in love with Africa. It happened when the Navy sent him to Africa for three weeks. The native people there quickly developed a strong relationship with Gerald (he loved people) and did not want him to leave. They begged him to stay and told him he was supposed to be their king. He had to leave them, but promised to come back one day. He never forgot that experience and talked about returning to see the people, but then he died unexpectedly.

God is so good to those who belong to him and have served him while on earth. My husband was involved in prison ministry for several years and loved to go and share with those who had no hope. What a reward God gave him!

Now he can live like a real chief and I am blessed every day to know it. It changed my life to know that Heaven is so real and that we are still remembered by our loved ones. It should not only give hope to us, but we can know that we will be rewarded for the things we do for our Lord".

CHAPTER FIVE

THE PORTAL

Another fantastic trip to Heaven was when I was allowed to tour a wondrous place they call The Portal. This is the place where all of Heaven can come to view earth. There were angels present as well as the Redeemed. The immensity of the place left me speechless, I could not even see the end walls. However, there were some columns near where I was walking that looked to be about 60 feet high. The detail of the embellishments had to be done by a master craftsman.

I finally approached the portal itself, which was magnificent. It seemed that when you walked up to it, you were looking over a balcony. The carvings on the rails and posts were finely detailed and wonderful to touch. The atmosphere inside was charged with excitement and at the same time, you were filled with awe. The light inside the structure was somewhat subdued, so that your attention was drawn to the portal and your viewing would not be interfered with. As always, the presence of God saturated everything and everyone. This was overwhelming to me, but perhaps that was because I was not a permanent resident. It is always difficult to focus on one thing in Heaven, because you do not just experience what you are seeing, and there are always aromas present together with indescribable music. It stirs you and all you can do is begin to declare God's goodness.

All the people were wearing their gowns and robes. The gowns were a brilliant white, but the robes were very different from each other. They were designed and embellished according to your level of 'reward' and service to the Lord; and some were so glorious that they could hang in an art gallery. This is one of the places in Heaven where it is requested that everyone come dressed alike. I feel that it promotes a sense of unity among all those coming to view, pray and cheer for their loved ones on earth.

It was extremely exciting to be there and I shall never forget the expressions of love, joy, surprise and victory I saw on the faces of the people. They were allowed to see significant events in their family's lives, such as marriages, births, celebrations and especially when they accepted Jesus as their Savior. How good of God to bless them, so that they can still be a part of the lives of those they left on earth.

Many people were leaning forward, whispering and gesturing to those that had accompanied them to view. There were hundreds present at the time I visited, but everyone saw something different – it is one of the wonders of Heaven – to have the ability to show everyone their specific families on earth all at the same time! There would be normal conversation, until someone on earth became a Christian, and then there was wild rejoicing and celebration. Everyone would congratulate the family whose loved one had come to believe in Jesus. It is the most exciting thing that happens at the portal.

Another exciting event is when a loved one comes home to Heaven. As soon as they realize that they are on their way, they race out to the Gate to greet them.

After viewing for what seemed to be an hour (it is very difficult to judge time by earth standards), I was instantly taken back to earth. It was almost impossible to go back to my 'normal' earthly duties after experiencing something supernatural like the portal. It is mentioned in the bible in Hebrews 12:1, where it talks about the 'great cloud of witnesses'. Remember now, we are always being watched!

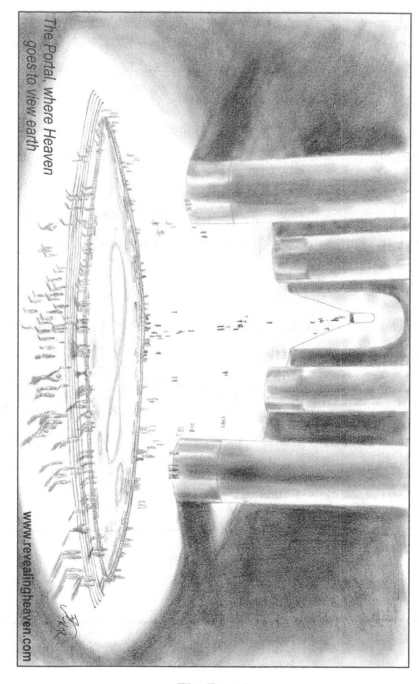

The Portal, where Heaven goes to view earth

www.revealingheaven.com

The Portal

CHAPTER SIX

THE FACE OF A CHILD –
HEAVEN'S NURSERIES

This chapter is somewhat bittersweet. Sweet because that is what babies are and they are kept in one of the most beautiful places I have ever visited in Heaven. Bitter because it is one of the most populated places in Heaven, thanks to the abortion clinics' business over the past 40 years. How accountable are we all for the mass abuse of these tiny babies? They are human lives swept under the carpet and remembered no more. Heaven knows how many of their lives were shredded, they know, because they have ALL of them there! Not a one was lost or discarded by our Heavenly Father.

Only because of His great mercy and Christ's blood is there forgiveness and healing available for this sin. Even the children, when grown to the age of a toddler, go through a ceremony where they receive Jesus and forgive the ones who took their lives. Yes, they know who their parents are and they are conscious of what happened to them when they first arrive in Heaven. They do not understand why they were not wanted, but they do forgive.

These nurseries hold all the babies which are miscarried or aborted. They are received by Jesus and He heals the wounds of their hearts. They are cared for by angelic beings who sing to them as they rock them in their arms. The breath of God nourishes them as they grow ever so slowly. Because of the goodness of God, a 20 year old mother could miscarry her baby and 50 years later die and go to Heaven; her baby would only be around 3 years old (in earth years). She is given her baby when she arrives and she gets to raise it. How wonderful for all the parents who thought they had completely lost that privilege!

The mercy of God allows the same thing for those who have aborted their babies, then repent and come to know Christ and make it to Heaven. For this reason alone, a second chance to hold your child in your arms and love and raise it as your own; wouldn't you want to make it there? Many will and they can experience the joy of watching their child (once destroyed and now restored) grow and become a happy, complete being! God desires this restoration in families.

Rahmee, an Angel from Heaven's nurseries

www.revealingheaven.com

Rahmee and Precious

This illustration is of the angel, **Rahmee,** and a baby named **Precious**, who was miscarried in 2006. This baby girl was wanted very badly by the parents and one day she will be restored to them, because they have received Jesus as their Savior. She will be treated like a princess until their arrival in Heaven. There will be many surprised women, who did not know they had miscarried a baby, because it was so early in the pregnancy. What a shock when they arrive and find a little 'package' waiting for them.

The facilities where these babies are cared for are very beautiful. There are arched ceilings with openings at the top which cause the rooms to be bathed in a warm peachy glow. Flowers are growing right out of the walls and tiny birds come and perch on the branches to sing for the babies. The babies 'beds' have the appearance of beautiful sea shells that come out from niches in the wall. Every baby's name is etched in the wall above them; embellished onto lovely ribbons if it is a girl and on stately shields if they are boys. If you have a baby in Heaven and haven't named it, please do so. Not only does it show Heaven you accept the fact that your baby lives there, but your child knows you cared enough to give it a name. If you didn't know the gender of your baby you can pick a girl name and a boy name and the appropriate name will be given. Or, you may choose a name that would be suitable for both.

Some of the angels appear to be male and some female but they all wore soft ivory gowns with pale colored sashes. They held the 'tiny' babies (some only inches long) in the palm of their hands and the bigger ones against their chests. As they sang to them, the breath of God nourished their little spirits. Even though these babies are tiny, they are different than the babies here, because they do not necessarily need to sleep. They do rest, but they also play. They already have the ability to 'know' things and they can communicate. They are raised in the perfect love of God and joy is an automatic part of their lives. It was a most beautiful place, filled with the peace of God. Their little faces reflect the Glory of God and they will know Him as we all should know Him.

Nursery wall

There are other places in Heaven for the older toddlers and children where they can play and learn. One place allows them to play games with the animals and actually slide down rainbows. Some of the landscape in the children's area is similar to different parts of earth, so they will be in familiar surroundings while they adapt to being in Heaven. It is a fun and exciting thing to be a child and live in Heaven. There will never be rejection, pain, illness or loneliness in their lives. Family members come to see them often and eventually, when they are big enough, are sent home with them to await the arrival of their parents. Please be sure to make the right choice with your life. Your children are waiting!

CHAPTER SEVEN

ENTERTAINMENT–IT WAS DESIGNED BY GOD FOR OUR PLEASURE.

This will probably be one of the most surprising chapters of the book, because not even I expected to find any of the following places in Heaven. Most of these things would be beyond our imagination to exist there, even though we should have expected God to create things for our enjoyment. The word does say…if we delight ourselves in Him, He will give us the desires of our heart; and fun would certainly be somewhere on that list. Since God is the supreme Creator, He chose to do just that, create FUN for his people. I will describe what it was like to visit three of these places.

The Rush

I shared earlier, in Chapter Four, about the amusement park I saw when God took me to heaven and showed Maurissa with her

Great Grandfather. The sketch I did was very simple and did not show the tremendous gates that welcomed you into the Park. They are always open and are not used in any way as a security measure. There is absolutely no reason to have 'security' of any kind in Heaven. There are no thieves, nor any danger of anyone vandalizing anything. The gates are merely used as a 'landmark' to show the entrance way to the Park. The gates were very ornate, gold and were embellished with the color purple. They rose to a height of approximately 20 feet and were banked on either side with the most glorious flowers I had ever seen. Flowers were also growing on either side of the path leading up to the gates. The sky above me was a soft blue and had peach and gold streaks going across it.

As I walked along the path I was again overwhelmed at experiencing this supernatural dimension. Light seems to come from everywhere and everything. There are NO shadows! I know that sounds unbelievable, but it is a fact – there are NO shadows in Heaven. It is also impossible to go anywhere without music suddenly 'appearing' somewhere close by. Yes, I did say 'appearing' because; music is more than just a sound. It has colors, sometimes in the shape of ribbons and sometimes those ribbons even have the words of the music being played. Worship happens continuously in Heaven and can be joined in by anyone who wishes to do so. Angelic beings and the Redeemed many times join in together. It is hard to resist becoming a part of a beautiful melody as it floats above you on the way to the Throne Room. All worship goes there and becomes a 'sweet' aroma to the Father. It actually has a tangible presence and many times also carry with it certain sweet or spicy aromas.

As I continued along the path towards the gate, I could hear people both laughing and screaming. I could also hear the whizzing sound of the cars racing down the track of the roller coaster. The cars on the track had the appearance of huge bullets without a top on them and they had no wheels. I still do not know how they raced about on the track without wheels, perhaps they rode on a cushion of light. As I came closer, I could see the expressions on the people's faces. Some were laughing and shouting, while others were screaming at the top of their voices. They were definitely having FUN. There was music coming from somewhere in the Park, although it seemed to be coming from everywhere – it is hard to explain.

I could see many other rides close by and in the distance. I don't know how big the park was, but there seemed to be no end to it. I was tickled to see that not only *people* were riding the 'Rush', but *angelic beings* were also enjoying it. I don't know how they kept their wings from flapping, as the roller coaster was going at a ter-rific speed. When they reached the peak and were about to plummet, everyone including the angels, raised there hands high over their heads and screamed all the way down. It was GREAT! There is no chance of injury, so things can move at a much greater speed in Heaven. There were sections of the roller coaster that had no track and the cars actually 'leapt' to the other side. I don't think there is much chance of seeing that in one of earth's parks! I am sure every teenager who comes here would love to live in this neighborhood.

There were many groups of people entering the park and going to the various rides. The best part is there is NO fee, not ever; and you can ride as often as you want. The vivid colors I saw on the stands and the rides themselves will take your breath away (of course, up there you don't need to breathe). It makes it difficult to not use our 'earthly' terms when speaking about a supernatural place. There were places to win awesome prizes, eat delicious food (the aromas were bombarding my senses every moment I was there) and fascinating shows to see. There was nothing disgusting, grotesque or fearful anywhere in the Park, but weird, wild and mind-blowing is a good way to describe other things that go beyond our imagination!

One such place is called "Fly By" and is designed to let anyone who is brave enough, learn to fly. As I mentioned previously, no one gets wings when you come to Heaven, but there is a place you can 'fly'. It is so much fun to watch people, especially the 'beginners'. They look like Peter Pan wannabes, or they look like they are trying to 'swim' through the air. There is stadium seating available for those who want to observe their family or friends. There is a separate area for intermediate and advanced flyers, but you do not go there unless you have really developed this skill. I am sure there are many young people who would love the chance to have a try at it.

There were so many other choices that I could probably write a book on this place alone. I cannot begin to even describe some of the incredible things God put there for us to enjoy. It was a glorious place designed by our Father to thrill and delight His children of all ages!

Heaven's Reality Theaters

In the Summer of 1996 while I was washing dishes in my kitchen, the Lord and Holy Spirit came in, spoke to me and said, "Go and sit down, I want to take you and show you Heaven's movie theaters". I responded with, "There are movie theaters in Heaven?" "Yes", He answered, "We call them 'reality theaters' and earth has nothing like them". I went and sat down and almost instantly I was in Heaven walking towards a spectacular large building. Even though it is always light in Heaven, the bright neon type lights emanating from this building could be seen for miles. Beautiful brilliant colors and contemporary music streamed from this place. Many people and even some angels were heading towards the entrance of the theaters.

Almost everyone was part of a group of either family and/or friends. They seemed filled with expectancy and were definitely looking forward to going to the movies. There were no ticket booths like on earth, so we all just went through the doors into what appeared to be the far end of huge lobby area. I proceeded to follow a family of three; a father, mother and daughter. They took the hallway to the left and I followed a little behind them. I was not sure where I was going, so thought I would hang back and see what happened. We were approaching some double doors which appeared to take us into the main seating area. The father and daughter went in through those doors, but to my surprise the mother continued down the hallway and just before I passed through the double doors behind her family, I saw her go through a single door a little further down from us.

I did not think much about it, because I was too busy taking in my surroundings. The theater was done in what we would call modern décor. The design of the seats was fantastic and when you sat in them, they molded themselves to fit everyone's unique shape. They were the most comfortable seats I ever sat in, it was as if 'comfort' came up and wrapped itself around you. The strange thing was the fact that I did not see anything that looked like a screen. Suddenly, the whole wall directly in front of us appeared to turn into liquid form and then became solid before our very eyes; it was the screen. How strange, but it was about to get even stranger.

The lights, which seemed to be coming from wide strips built into the walls, dimmed and the movie started. The family I had followed in was sitting directly in front of me. I was wondering why the mother had not yet joined them, when they began to laugh somewhat nervously. My eyes went to the screen and I was thrilled to see the movie title come across, "The Sound of Music"; it was one of my all time favorites. What happened next though, really shocked me. Instead of Julie Andrews running across the hilltop, it was the 'missing' mother of the family I had followed in. They clapped excitedly for a brief moment and whispered together, nodding their heads towards the screen. I immediately wondered, "Why is she playing the leading role?" The Holy Spirit said, "This is her appointed time, which is why her family is here; so they can enjoy her debut". My mind was trying to comprehend His words, but all that came out was, "That is not possible, she just arrived and walked in that other door. How can she be in a movie that hasn't actually been made yet?" The Holy Spirit laughed and said, "It doesn't have to be 'made', it is captured. Come and I will show you".

Instantly, I was no longer in the theater, but on the hilltop watching the mother singing the opening tune of the movie. I wanted to pinch myself, because I just did not get it! How is this possible? I saw none of the normal equipment used on movie lots and only two individuals were present other than the mother and me. One was holding a strange apparatus the size of a hairbrush which seemed to be supplying all of the music and sound effects for the movie. The other individual had an even stranger device which I can only guess, captures the movie and simultaneously sends it back to the theater screen. I looked around and the scenery, which was real, not manufactured as props, was exactly like it was in the original movie. In the distance, I could see the convent with its bell tower. The meadows were beautifully green with small white flowers dotting the hillsides, and the valleys with meandering streams looked like something from an artist's canvas. Finally, it dawned on me, "How absolutely wonderful, you can go see the movie or be in it"! Instantly I was again sitting in the theater. Who would have ever imagined such a thing; it really was a 'reality' theater. When the movie ended, the mother joined her family and they all went off to celebrate her movie debut.

I thought that would be the end of my tour, but not yet. I followed another family; father, mother and their two sons to another theater. This time only the mother went in to be seated and the father with his two sons proceeded on down the hall. I went in and sat down, this time waiting with anticipation. It did not take long for the movie to start and this time it was a western. Much to both my and the mother's delight, her husband and two sons appeared on the screen, riding on horseback out across a prairie. They were dressed like real cowboys and speeding away to catch up to another rider in front of them. I could hardly believe my eyes, it was John Wayne and he had blazing pistols in both hands as he rode after some villain. I embarrassed myself by letting out a loud laugh and exclaimed at the same time, "It's the Duke, he made it to Heaven!" Everyone else in the theater laughed at my outburst. I was surprised they could hear me, because usually I was an unseen observer.

When the movie ended, I was taken right back to my kitchen table. I don't know how long in Heaven's 'time span' I was there, but in earth time it was only a few seconds. This would be the end, except I was taken again just a few months ago. I was sitting at my computer thinking about the time I had gone to see the movies; when suddenly, I was there again. This time an angel was escorting me across the lot to the building. He said, "We wanted you to visit the lobby area so you could tell how movies are advertised and how you sign up to be in them". "This is so exciting; I get to go twice and without even asking"!

As we entered the building, we were jostled by others also trying to enter. It looked like everyone in Heaven was there. Families and friends all coming together to either be in a movie or watch their loved ones fulfill their dream of acting. I was so absorbed watching the people that I started walking backwards and soon walked right into what appeared to be a battle going on all around me. I jumped, thinking I was being attacked. Then I realized that none of the swords being wielded were actually touching me. I stood, trans-fixed by the scene before me. It was then I realized I was standing in the middle of a scene from the original 'Star Wars'. Many of the movies on the earth are shown in Heaven, provided they meet Heaven's standards. Meaning, there would be no content displaying graphic violence, profane language, sensuality, and no spiritual darkness. More specifically, no movies that portray good witch-craft versus bad witchcraft. (There are no "good" evil people.) The action continued all around me when I finally understood that I was standing in a hologram and not something that was actually live. I ran outside the preview and saw many other such holograms taking place all over the lobby. This was their 'advertising' the angel had mentioned. Fantastic, I thought. You don't just view an upcoming movie, you can join into it! There were holograms on platforms, smaller ones on pedestals and some even on top of tables which people were sitting at in a nearby café.

I looked over to my right and saw a line of people waiting to use a device near the wall that looked similar to our ATMs. I knew they did not use money, so I came closer. It was some type of monitor where you could see which movies were going to be showing soon and what parts were left that you could take in the movie. I watched as two young girls (around 12 years old, earth years) signed up to be in a movie together. They were very excited about the whole thing and giggled continuously. When I turned back around, I was instantly sitting in front of my computer again. "WOW", I exclaimed. I loved it and I couldn't wait to tell someone what just happened. It is definitely exciting to be in Heaven, it is the place where the 'never dreamed of' things happen all the time!

This was so much fun, but it really made me consider that maybe Hollywood should adapt to Heaven's standards, because I don't think a lot of what they have been putting out lately would make it to Heaven. If you are an actor or actress and plan on going to Heaven you should consider the roles you accept down here if you want it shown up there. If you have accepted Christ as your Savior, at least now you know you can still have a future to use your gift in heaven.

If you do not accept Him and end up in Hell, you have NO future except to spend eternity in agony and fear. The only entertainment there is for the demons that torment you.

THE HALL OF NATIONS

The third place I visited was both fun and educational. They call it the Hall of the Nations and there were things to do both inside and outside. I was taken inside where there was a lobby area and people were greeted by a host or hostess. Sometimes I could not be sure if they (the greeters) were human or created beings. There are other created beings in Heaven that are not angels, or at least they do not have wings. They look very similar to us except if you look real close, you can see that they appear to be somewhat transparent. They are always friendly and always know you by name.

Running off from the lobby were many long hallways and all of them had people coming and going. I went down one of the annexes and stopped at what looked like some type of 'station' protruding out of the wall. Further down the hallway I saw literally dozens of these 'stations'. As I stepped towards it, a low stage-like platform rose up from the floor. It was round and looked like it was made of glass, but I don't believe it was. I stepped up onto the platform and immediately in front of me appeared a floor to ceiling mirror / monitor with reflective abilities. It was the color of burnished pewter and I could see myself in it. The monitor had a six inch modern looking (or we might call it 'futuristic') frame all the way around it and on the side it had two small scanning devices in the shape of an arrow pointing up and one pointing down. The whole device had a strange quality to it, in that you could see no 'seams' or any way of joining or holding the unit together. It amazed me!

I looked down the hallway and could see a young man who looked to be of 'Asian' decent stepping up onto one of the platforms. (In Heaven, the Redeemed are made up from all the nations). He was wearing a green tunic outfit, but was wearing no shoes. This tunic must be a normal piece of everyone's wardrobe, because I have seen it being worn all over Heaven in every type of style, color and fabric imaginable. I was watching to see what he would do next, when he reached forward and passed his hand over the top arrow on the frame. Immediately, a solid stream of light in the shape of a cylinder, poured over him. It was coming from a small dome in the ceiling above him and completely covered his entire being from head to toe. *What I saw happen next, completely floored me*. Right before my eyes, he was transformed from the Asian race to Bahamian!

Hall of Nations

95

Everything about him was different; his skin, his hair, his face and even his clothes. The only thing that remained the same was his body size and his eyes. I almost fell off my platform, but was able to regain my composure. "That is so cool", I said as I heard him laughing at himself. He also appeared transformed in the monitor on the wall. When he was done, he leaned forward, passed his hand over the down arrow and everything changed back as the light went off.

I quickly turned, leaned forward and touched my 'up' arrow. A second later, I was no longer Caucasian, but a female Aborigine (with blue eyes). It was quite a sight to see! As long as I stood within the cylinder of light my appearance did not change back; but if I extended my arm out beyond the light, that part of my body went back to it's original state. You could look down at yourself and not just 'see' you were different, but you could touch your skin and hair and 'feel' the difference. How marvelous, I never dreamed of anything like this being possible. I stared at myself for a few more moments and then passed my hand over the 'down' arrow and the light dissolved from around me and I was once again, back to my normal self.

Nothing could stop me from running to one station after another to see what I would become. The next one, I was an American Indian, then an Asian, then Dutch, Italian and before they took me back I was a Scottish lass. Each time you started as yourself, wearing your tunic outfit, except for me; I had on a t-shirt and jeans, and whatever ethnic group you became, you would be wearing the traditional or native dress that went with it. I would have liked to have kept the bagpipes, but maybe when I 'permanently' come home, I will learn to play them!

What a delightful thought, to be able to see and feel what it is like to step into the shoes of another. There are definitely 'supernatural' things to do up there and I only experienced a few of them.

CHAPTER EIGHT

MEMORIALS OF MAN

Your giving and kindness is remembered forever!

In this chapter I will reveal what I was told and shown about the memorials that man builds in Heaven and how they are 'before' God forever.

There is a story in the Book of Acts, Chapter 10, about a Gentile named Cornelius. He was a good man and gave much money to the poor. He had a kind heart and was known throughout the region. Cornelius was not just building a reputation on earth, but in Heaven too. So much so, that God sent an Angel to Cornelius with these words: (KJ) "Your prayers and your alms have come up for a memorial before God" or from the Everyday Bible, New Century Version: "He (God) has seen that you give to the poor and remembers you".

And from the Living Bible: "Your prayers and your charities have not gone unnoticed by God". God was so impressed with Cornelius's goodness towards the poor that He wanted to make sure he had an opportunity to hear the gospel. He even prepared Peter ahead of time (through a vision) so he would not reject him because he was a Gentile.

We cannot get into Heaven with our works, only accepting Jesus qualifies you for that. However, when we live our lives the same way as Cornelius (unselfishly), we too build a memorial in Heaven with our generosity. There are many people here on earth, some are very well known, that have built fantastic memorials in Heaven. Some are so big that they look like small cities; with large fountains, gardens and benches to sit on. There are galleries where you can go inside and actually view some of the kind acts they have performed. Their names are always displayed on some type of plaque or on the monument itself. If you know someone who has a giving heart and they continually help others, they probably have one of these memorials. It doesn't matter where you go in Heaven, these memorials are everywhere.

Two memorials in particular caught my eye. One was made from mother-of-pearl and it shone brightly against the landscape. It was the size of a city park, with beautiful waterfalls that ended into the basin of a large fountain. All around the base wall of the fountain were figurines of children in various stages of play. Their little faces filled with delight and expectation. The upper wall of the fountain had the most beautiful butterflies engraved into it. They were so real that I expected them to take flight at any moment. At the very top of the fountain was a scrolled plaque which read: "A MEMORIAL FOR YOUR LOVE AND KINDNESS TO THE FORGOTTEN CHILDREN OF THE WORLD".

The detail work on the fountain must have been done by one of Heaven's best artisans. Flowers were in bloom everywhere and the fragrance from them stirred your senses; some of them cascaded down the walls that surrounded the extensive gardens. Peacocks strutted across the grounds and were perching on some of the smaller fountains which ran alongside the wall. What a beautiful place to have been formed from someone's labors of love towards the needy!

This memorial belongs to a precious Christian woman who is often maligned by both the secular world and even by some of those in leadership who profess to know Christ. This does not please the Father, but rather saddens Him. He highly honors her in heaven for efforts. She has remembered the orphans and the abandoned of the world and is doing something about it! Watch your words and do not touch God's anointed. You may not approve of them personally and if you truly feel they have made mistakes, then pray for them. The bible says if they are producing good fruit with their lives on behalf of Christ, then they are 'for' Him and not against Him. Do not let your own words delay or defeat what God has for you by speaking against any of His children.

The other memorial I saw was just as spectacular, but very different in design. It too started with a large fountain, but this one had a transparent bridge which crossed over top of it. It had a more 'modern' design to it and seemed to be filled with this beautiful blue light. As you entered the bridge and began to pass over this huge fountain, you look down into smaller pools that were part of its design and instead of seeing your own reflection, you saw the faces of all those who had been helped in some way by this individual. The things you viewed, had actually taken place at some time and had been captured by Heaven and secured into this memorial. Not only could you see the expression on the people's faces, but you could hear the very words of gratitude they spoke to this individual.

Masses of roses and white Baby's Breath surrounded this fountain and went up the sides of the huge columns that were a part of its structure. Platforms came out from either side of the fountain where at various times, Heaven's symphonies would come and play concerts for the enjoyment of all those present. The glorious music could be heard for some distance and all those who heard it would stop and give glory to God for His goodness to others.

Near the fountain area were multiple areas for sitting and fellowshipping with others, which is a favorite pastime of this individual. They really love people and the only reward asked was what they saw in the faces of the people when they had helped them. Many of these people were extremely needy and had their lives changed forever, because of the efforts of this person.

There are areas where small children can come and enjoy playing on a variety of unusual playthings. Some I had never seen before, like the bubble balls. A child would walk up into this domed structure which had a hole at the top and as they stood there, a large bubble would encase them and they would float out and start bouncing off their friends' bubbles. They would laugh and shout as they floated about. When they tired of it, they simply 'popped' their bubble and would return to the ground.

How wonderful that not only was this individual bringing happiness to children on earth, but in Heaven also. God's love had been expressed through this person, time and time again. They did not even realize they had been influenced by the Spirit of God to do a lot of these 'acts of kindness'. They were wealthy in their own right and could have been selfish, but chose instead to use their life for the betterment of others. They were never prejudice against any particular group, but treated everyone fairly as the bible says we should. As a result, this magnificent memorial was built with their love. It would be a shame if the one who built this memorial, never got to see it. *As I said before, the memorial does not guarantee entry into Heaven, if they do not accept Christ; the memorial will remain but they will never see it!*

Some people may try to argue that God would have nothing in heaven that relates to the sinner; however, Cornelius and his family got saved after the angel came and spoke. This is proof that God not only hears the prayer of the unsaved, but even recognizes the good things they do for the poor and needy. God desires to draw close to us, that is why He created man; so that He could have a family to have fellowship with.

One important lesson God taught me was to never judge the heart of man; only He knows what is in it. He decides who goes, because He is the only judge! Many will make last-minute confessions and there will be many people in Heaven that we never expected to see there.

The Throne Room

revealingheaven.com

Throne Room

Will your life build a memorial before the Throne of God? It is a most Holy place and all things must be passed through the fire before being presented. Even though there is dancing, singing and celebrating, it is still a place of reverence and 'awe'. Many times the Glory is so heavy, no one can stand in it; and they fall prostrate before the throne. It is a place that is always available to all who dwell in Heaven. The Father welcomes any who wish to see Him. Jesus and the Father and Holy Spirit are one, in that they have the ability to go 'in' and 'out' of each other. They think alike, feel alike and love alike; and are all "equally" HOLY! When you pray, you are talking to all of them. When you worship, you are honoring all of them. Develop a lifestyle of prayer and worship that is how you pursue an 'intimacy' with them. They desire it, more than you know! THE PURPOSE OF LIFE IS TO BE A PART OF THEIR FAMILY.

CHAPTER NINE

No Party in Hell, Only demons rejoice

This chapter is a continuation of Chapter Two where I talked about Hell. It is a TERRIBLE place, full of fear and torment and NO WAY of escape. Hell was never intended for man, but was made for the devil and his fallen angels. God is love and desires that none should perish; but because He is holy, no sin can abide in His presence. If you do not repent from sin, you cannot come to heaven and the only other choice you get is Hell. Who would want to be separated from their loved ones for all eternity?

I was actually in prayer one evening when I was taken and shown Hell. No one who has been there could ever forget the horror of that place. I am grateful that I did not get the full effect, in that I only observed it and did not personally experience torture or the searing heat from the flames. I know that others who have been there were literally dropped in and they did experience the pain, suffering and worst of all, the separation from God. Believe me, seeing it was bad enough for me.

That was one of the times I was actually told where I was being taken and for what purpose. God knew when I told people about Heaven, I would need to warn them about Hell too. Many people do not believe in Hell, but that will not keep them from going there. Can you imagine a person living a 'good' life and because they rejected Christ, end up in such a place? It would be like having your worst nightmare come true. Your only company would be demons who hate you. They hate you, because they hate God and we are made in His image. Their greatest pleasure is tearing someone apart, literally.

The screams were almost unbearable to me and I knew there would never be any mercy in Hell. Fear ruled there and even if you had a momentary reprieve from the demonic torment until it started all over again, the mental torment never stops.

You may have heard the saying, "Let's party in Hell"! Well, the only ones who do that are the demonic beings. They rejoice every time a new victim arrives. If two friends should arrive together, one will be dragged away and the other must watch in helpless horror as their friend is shredded before their eyes; unable to answer their screams for help.

Sometimes, people are thrown into pits filled with fire and small animal-like demons bite you continuously and you will feel all the pain as wound after wound appears on your body. The heat is unquenchable as it produces huge blisters all over your body and the smell of scorched flesh is everywhere.

Another form of torture used in hell is the stone tomb. They entomb you in a space barely high enough to stand and not wide enough to kneel or sit. It is the blackest black you have ever experienced and it is bitter cold. Small spider demons that have human heads crawl all over you as they scream blasphemies nonstop. The sound pierces your head again and again until you think you will go insane.

Not only does your exhausted body have no way to lie down; but if you try to relax your legs, they scrape against the sharp needle-like stones on the sides of the tomb. It is agony to have no rest and no water for your dehydrated body which is already suffering starvation pangs. You wish you could cease to exist, so the suffering will stop; but it never does.

My viewing of Hell was brief, but it doesn't take long to realize that no one will want to end up there. People say they do not believe a merciful loving God could send anyone to Hell. ***They are right, He does not send anyone there; they make that choice themselves***. God set a mandate that ONLY the blood of His Son could give you entrance to Heaven, not because He wants all others to go to hell; but it was necessary to keep hell, evil, sin and darkness out of Heaven and Eternity FOREVER!

We must guard our hearts so that once saved, you do not sin against God. It is possible to accept Christ and start out living right, but then we get pulled away from God either by our own selfish lusts or we are enticed by the things the devil has planted in this world to destroy us and steal our destiny. Some of these 'traps' the enemy uses are drugs, alcohol, immorality, greed and hate. One of the devil's favorite sinful deceptions to trap people into is homosexuality, which is a LIE, as God does not make anyone in that image. We are made in the image of God and there is no homosexuality in Him. The devil convinces people they are 'made' that way by using perverted unclean spirits (even from a young age). In reality he has twisted the image of God into a lie because he wants to steal and destroy the destiny of those individuals. But God desires that they know the TRUTH so they can repent and be free! Other traps the enemy sets are witchcraft (there is NO good witchcraft, it is ALL dangerous) and devil worship.

Those are the obvious ones, but there are also the not so obvious; and one of them is *unforgiveness*. The bible clearly says, "If you do not forgive, you will NOT be forgiven". Please do not let this hideous sin be found in you. Be quick to forgive if someone asks and do not harden your heart. Even if you accepted Christ, lived a good life and helped the poor; all wonderful things according to the bible, but harbored unforgiveness (a hate so strong you would desire that they die and even on your deathbed you would refuse to forgive them), You Will be judged by HEAVEN.

Do not think that by simply saying a 'sinner's prayer it seals you forever to go to Heaven. You must sincerely mean it and even though salvation is free, that does not give you a license to live any way you want to. If you then continue to live a life of sin and disregard God's commandments, you never really had a true conversion!

If you need help in order to forgive someone, make a decision with your Will to forgive (even if your flesh does not feel like it), God is faithful and you will be free from unforgiveness. Anyone who goes to hell will NEVER be free and never feel peace, kindness or love again. Even their future has been planned for them; it will be spent burning in the Lake of Fire for all eternity! If anyone you know went there, they are screaming out to God to not let you come there! Please choose Christ while there is yet time!

I would like to make mention of something the Father assured me of, He NEVER sends children to hell. I saw millions of children (of all ages) playing in Heaven, awaiting the arrival of family members.

Until one comes to the Age of Accountability, (not a number age) but a clear understanding that you are making a choice for good or evil; that will affect your eternity. You will KNOW that you had a choice, considered it and made a decision with your free will choosing evil over God.

CHAPTER TEN

MAKING YOUR ELECTION SURE, SO YOU CAN MAKE IT TO HEAVEN.

This chapter will clearly explain how to get saved, or as some call it 'born again'. What it means is you will no longer be separated from God by sin, but you become a part of His family by accepting Jesus as your Savior and, therefore will go to Heaven when you die. There is scripture which explains it all, John 3:16, 17; "For God so loved the world that He gave His only begotten Son that whosoever believeth in Him shall not perish, but have everlasting life. For God sent not His son into the world that it might be condemned, but that the world through Him might be saved." It is that simple and it is a free gift. **You must confess your sins, recognize that Jesus is the Son of the living God and receive the sacrifice of Jesus dying on the cross, so you could be forgiven. He is**

the only way to the Father and the ONLY way to Heaven. Don't wait until you 'clean up' your life, He will take you just as you are; receive Him then He will change you from the inside, out!

Once you have repented of your sins, you become a new individual and the 'old' you passes away. This means your heart has been changed and it now desires the things of God and not the wicked things they once did. Any sins you were guilty of have now been removed. In order for you to grow spiritually, you must begin to read the Word of God (the Bible). It also helps to develop relationships with those who have known God for some time and can help you pursue a strong Christian walk. If you get connected with a local ministry, they can offer practical guidance and counsel to help you find your destiny and purpose God made you for.

The next step (although not required to go to Heaven) is to be baptized in water, which is an outward sign of the inward change that has taken place in your life. It signifies that we have 'died' with Christ and now resurrected, have become a new person. Most local churches hold baptismal services on a regular basis and would be glad to welcome you into the family of God by baptizing you. The first church, as explained in the book of Acts, baptized all new converts.

Then, if you really want to be empowered (again, not a requirement to go to Heaven), you should pursue the Holy Spirit to take control of your life by seeking the in-dwelling of the Holy Spirit. This empowers you as it did the apostles in the book of Acts. I would advise reading the entire book to see what a difference this made in their lives. You become more sensitive to hear the inner voice of God speaking to you and you become bold. The Holy Spirit was sent to be a guide and a comforter! When the great outpouring mentioned in the Foreword of this book takes place, many will simultaneously be filled with the Holy Spirit and the results will be miraculous!

Everyone who professes to be a follower of Christ should represent His character. He came because He loved all people and therefore, we should do the same. We cannot love the 'sin' people fall into, but we can 'love' them to Christ. Read the book of Galatians to learn how brothers and sisters in Christ should treat each other. We should all strive to have a good report recorded in Heaven.

Jesus desires you to experience victory over sin every day of your life. The word of God says, "Whatsoever is born of God overcomes the world; and this is the victory that overcomes the world, even our faith" (1 John 5:4). The devil will bring temptation to you, but you do not have to do it. Jesus can help you win every time, because "Greater is He that is in you, than he that is in the world" (1 John 4:4). When you feel that pressure to give in to sin just run to Him and He will help you. If you do fall and sin the worst thing you can do is try to hide it, confess your sin quickly and receive His forgiveness. If you hide sin the devil will use it against you and then condemnation will come. The longer you wait, the harder it will be to repent. His forgiveness is available for us all and His blood can make the vilest sinner FREE!

I not only know that Christ died for our sins and poured out His blood before the throne of God, but I have seen it! I will now share one of the most unusual and unforgettable experiences I have ever had. It was April 1998 and I was at the evening church service. At this time I had been seeking a deeper relationship with the Father and had spent many evenings worshipping and interceding at my home. I was 'hungry' for more of the Lord and when you get to that place in your life, He will make sure you get it.

We had been worshipping for about thirty minutes and then Pastor stopped and called certain people down for prayer. He asked for anyone who was in the full time ministry, whether they were licensed ministers or lay ministers. I knew God had told me I would one day be in full time marketplace ministry, but resisted, because that time had not yet arrived. Pastor laid hands on those who had gone forward, prayed for them and released them to return to their seats. I could feel the glory of God in the sanctuary and I knew that angels were present. I felt the Holy Spirit impressing me that I should have gone down to be prayed for, so I said to Him, "If Pastor says, there is still one more person who needs to come, then I will go". The very next moment, my Pastor said those very words, so I went forward.

The closer I got to the front, the stronger the glory of God became. It became hard to breathe and I began to feel heat all around me. They had an usher stand behind me, because sometimes when the power of God is released into you, you can actually go down. When Pastor laid hands on me, I felt 'fire' go all the way up through my body. It was so powerful that not only did it knock me back, but the usher got thrown back also. God used the hands of my Pastor to release this fire into my spirit. It went through my entire being, burning up anything that was not of God. The walls of my heart were wiped clean of any desire for the world, any past bad memories and then went up through my head to cleanse my thought life. I was now a pure vessel, set aside for the Father's use. I had been baptized with fire!

I only remember going down to the floor and my body began to shake violently. I was not injured in any way, but was consumed by the Glory and that was how my body reacted to it. I vaguely remember someone covering me and walking away. Later I found out that I shook through the remainder of the service, the whole time lying on the floor down front. Pastor knew God was doing something and would not allow anyone to touch or move me. They actually locked me in the church and left a security person there to call my family when I was able to leave. My daughter told me the next morning that it was she who had left a note with our home phone number stuffed up my sleeve. She had waited until almost midnight, but I was still lying there shaking. What she did not know was where I had been taken by the Spirit of God.

When I hit the floor, seconds later the angel of the Lord took me (my spirit) and left this earth. In all the times I have gone to Heaven it is always 'in an instant' and I do not feel I have traveled at all. I am just here and a second later I am somewhere in Heaven. It was different this time, because suddenly it felt like we were moving in 'warp' speed. I actually saw millions of lights coming at me, just like you would see in a movie. We traveled for some time and suddenly we stopped and I felt my feet hit the ground. I opened my eyes and I instantly knew I was not in Heaven. When I realized where I was my heart caught in my throat, for I was standing outside the tomb of Jesus and the stone had already been rolled away. "Oh God", I said, "what am I seeing?"

I heard someone crying and turned and I saw a beautiful girl with something under her arm. She looked to be around nineteen years old and had long black hair. She looked into the tomb and saw the angels, who asked her why she was crying. She said, "They have taken away my Lord and I don't know where they put Him." Just then Mary turned and saw Jesus but did not recognize Him as she thought He was the gardener because he was smelling the flowers outside the tomb. She asked him if he had taken Jesus. Then Jesus said, "Mary." She ran towards him, her face now radiant with joy, as she called out, "Rabboni." (I believe that means 'teacher' in the Jewish language.) Jesus said to her, "Do not hang on to me Mary, because I have to go to my Father first. Tell the others where I am going, to my Father and your Father." She ran off to tell the others what Jesus said.

As soon as she left a large company of angels appeared in the sky and as Jesus rose to meet them, I followed. It was a breathtaking site as we rose up together, I will NEVER forget it. I did not care if anyone ever believed me; this would always be a 'divine' time in my life. The angels were flanking out and around Jesus, as we continued up through the heavens. Even though the atmosphere around us would have normally been dark, the brilliance from the Glory around Jesus lit up the entire area. We passed through the second heaven with no interference and proceeded towards a light that looked brighter than the sun.

As we entered the third heaven, which is where God's home is, thousands upon thousands of angels had come to greet Jesus upon His return from the grave. They escorted us through the gates and towards the Throne Room. The site I saw next is hard to explain, and even as I write about it, the Glory I felt then rests upon me now! There was an innumerable amount of angels prostrate on the floor as Jesus walked towards the throne and His Father. The angel of the Lord had been carrying a beautiful vase with him the entire time and now he was offering it to Christ as He stepped before His Father.

In front of us was a low type of alter and on it was a gorgeous runner whose threads that bound it together seemed to be alive. Gold, silver, purple, red, and green were the moving colors in this piece of fabric. I could hardly stand; the power emanating from the throne was so great. Lightning was shooting forth and it sounded like great thunder, as the Father raised His right hand.

Then suddenly, there was absolute silence as Jesus took the vase and bent over the altar. Just before He began to pour out His blood, I saw a word appear on the cloth in front of Him. It said, 'Fear', but as the blood hit it, I heard a sound like water hitting a hot pan, 'SSSSSSSS'; immediately the word evaporated. One by one, words appeared on the cloth and every time the blood would dissolve them. Words like, 'Hate, Disease, Grief, Murder, Homosexuality, Insanity, Adultery, Pain', and many more; each time being dissolved by the blood of Jesus. When the last word; 'DEATH', appeared the blood hit it and it was gone forever. God stood up and raised both arms, He shouted, "YES! It is finished"! Everyone in the Throne Room shouted and danced with joy. Jesus had accomplished it, the supreme sacrifice had been made and the blood offering paid in full. The 'living' runner now containing Christ's precious blood would be kept forever upon the mercy seat of God. What a holy thing to experience, I am surprised I lived through it!

(I was then returned to the church)

It was around 5:00 a.m. before they could call my husband to come and get me; and he had to carry me out. I was not normal for about two weeks. I had many visions during that time and will share them another time. I truly know He paid the supreme price for all of us. **How can anyone refuse such Love?**

The Mercy Seat

revealingheaven.com

Mercy Seat

ETERNAL PLANNING, SALVATION IS FREE, BUT YOUR LIFE LIVED NOW, DETERMINES YOUR ETERNAL POSITION!

This chapter explains how your eternal position is determined and you are actually the one who decides it!

People do many types of planning in their lifetime; Vacation Plans, Homebuilding Plans, Savings Plans, College Fund Plans, Retirement Planning and even Estate Planning. The most important, but most overlooked planning is ETERNAL PLANNING. I am not talking about getting saved so you can make it to Heaven. I am talking about something beyond that. Your eternal position, which once set will never be changed. You can work towards it until you die, after that there is not much you can do. That means you find out what God's purpose is for the body of Christ (ruling and reigning in the spirit) and then accomplish it by using the authority over darkness that Christ gives us by choosing Him. On the earth our spiritual level of authority increases as we are willing and obedient to do what Christ asks and by pursuing an intimate relationship with Him. He has a destiny for all of us. You will either rule or reign with Christ in the new earth, or you will serve others.

Make sure your life counts for the Kingdom by releasing the Kingdom of God that is within you into the earth. Your reward will be to spend eternity ruling with Christ. You will never regret it! Please remember the Lord's prayer in Matthew 6.

CHAPTER TWELVE

THE FATHER'S LOVE LETTER

This beautiful blending of the Holy Scriptures is used with permission from Father Heart Communications.

My Child...

You may not know me, but I know everything about you...Psalm 139:1 I know when you sit down and when you rise up...Psalm 139:2 I am familiar with all your ways...Psalm 139:3 Even the very hairs on your head are numbered...Matthew 10:29-31 For you were made in my image...Genesis 1:27 In me you live and move and have your being...Acts 17:28 For you are my offspring...Acts 17:28 I knew you even before you were conceived...Jeremiah 1:4-5 I chose you when I planned creation...Ephesians 1:11-12 You were not a mistake, for all your days are written in my book ...Psalm 139:15-16 I determined the exact time of your birth and where you would live...Acts 17:26 You are fearfully and wonderfully made... Psalm 139:14 I knit you together in your mother's womb...Psalm

139:13 And brought you forth on the day you were born... Psalm 71:6 I have been misrepresented by those who don't know me... John 8:41-44 I am not distant and angry, but am the complete expression of love...1 John 4:16 And it is my desire to lavish my love on you... 1John 3:1 Simply because you are my child and I am your Father... 1John 3:1 I offer you more than your earthly father ever could...Matthew 7:11 For I am the perfect Father...Matthew 5:48 Every good gift that you receive comes from my hand...James 1:17 For I am your provider and I meet all your needs...Matthew 6:31-33 My plan for your future has always been filled with hope...Jeremiah 29:11 Because I love you with an everlasting love...Jeremiah 31:3 My thoughts toward you are countless as the sand on the seashore... Psalm 139:17-18 And I rejoice over you with singing...Zephaniah 3:17 I will never stop doing good to you...Jeremiah 32:40 For you are my treasured possession...Exodus 19:5 I desire to establish you with all my heart and all my soul...Jeremiah 32:41 And I want to show you great and marvelous things...Jeremiah 33:3 If you seek me with all your heart, you will find me...Deuteronomy 4:29 Delight in me and I will give you the desires of your heart...Psalm 37:4 For it is I who gave you those desires...Philippians 2:13 I am able to do more for you than you could possibly imagine...Ephesians 3:20 For I am your greatest encourager...2 Thessalonians 2:16-17 I am also the Father who comforts you in all your troubles...2Corinthians 1:3-4 When you are brokenhearted, I am close to you...Psalm 34:18 As a shepherd carries a lamb, I have carried you close to my heart... Isaiah 40:11 One day I will wipe away every tear from your eyes... Revelation 21:3-4 And I'll take away all the pain you have suffered on this earth...Revelation 21:3-4 I am your Father, and I love you even as I love my son, Jesus...John 17:23 For in Jesus, my love for you is revealed...John 17:26 He is the exact representation of my being...Hebrews 1:3 He came to demonstrate that I am for you, not against you...Romans 8:31 And to tell you that I am not counting your sins...2 Corinthians 5:18-19 Jesus died so that you and I could be reconciled ...2Corinthians 5:18-19 His death was the ultimate expression of my love for you...1 John 4:10 I gave up everything I loved that I might gain your love...Romans 8:31-32 If you receive the gift of my son Jesus, you receive me...1 John 2:23 And nothing

will ever separate you from my love again … Romans 8:38-39
Come home and I'll throw the biggest party heaven has ever seen …
Luke 15:7 I have always been Father, and will always be Father…
Ephesians 3:14-15 My question is…Will you be my child?… John
1:12-13 I am waiting for you……. Luke 15:11-32

…Love, Your Dad

Almighty God
This chapter was created by: Father Heart Communications
Copyright 1999 www.FathersLoveLetter.com

A FINAL NOTE FROM THE FATHER TO HIS BODY

Please **STOP** fighting each other. I made you all and I love you all. You were given different callings and anointing. **DO NOT** come against anyone who is doing My work. Do you not know that My Word says, 'Touch not my anointed'; and yet you despise and devour each other!

You are all **ONE** family and you will live that way in Heaven and throughout eternity. I did not separate you from each other; that is man's tradition. I am about to show up and interrupt a lot of those traditions because in these last days it is <u>crucial</u> that you all work together. The world will know you by your love for each other.

ARE YOU LOVING?

APPENDIX

1. **Question and Answer Section -**

A National Survey was done with over 400 people (from age 5 to 90) that asked one question: **"If you could ask God one question about Heaven, what would it be?"**

We have included 45 of those questions with answers.

2. **Suggested reading of related topics:**

"The Heaven's Opened", **by Anna Rountree**

"Kisses from Heaven", **by Melodee Nobles (Maurissa's Mother), soon to be released!**

3. **Scriptures concerning Heaven. I would encourage you to look them up and read them yourself.**

> **John 14:2 & 3**
> **I Corinthians 2:9**
> **II Corinthians 5:8**
> **Amos 3:7**
> **Matthew 25:41**
> **Hebrews 8:5**
> **Hebrews 12:1**

Acts 10:4
Psalms 9:17
Galatians 5:19 – 21
John 3:16

4. **Standing with Israel**

5. **About the Author**

6. **Statement of Faith**

7. **Contact Information**

SURVEY QUESTIONS
WITH ANSWERS

Trey, Age 6
Richmond, VA

Is there an art easel and a T-Rex in Heaven?

Yes, to both questions. Since I saw art galleries there, I am certain they would have easels to paint on. Also, there are representations of all animal life that God originally created. So, dinosaurs including the T-Rex, can be seen in the park area of Heaven, they are so tame that you can actually ride on them!

Brian, Age 11
Jacksonville, FL

Why isn't there night in Heaven?

God made the night on earth, so our physical body could be refreshed through sleep. In Heaven, we never need sleep, because our spiritual body doesn't get tired, so there is no need for night time. The Glory of God lights Heaven so there is no sun or moon but many times the sky changes with amazing shades of color not on this earth.

Krystina, Age 16
Florida

After you come to Heaven, can you come back to earth?

Sometimes, in rare circumstances, for only a moment in time, you are allowed to briefly return to earth and then immediately go back to Heaven (usually right after dying). This is not the norm and only God makes that decision, not you. No one's spirit continues to live on this earth after death, you either go live in Heaven or in hell; and NO one's spirit ever leaves hell until the Great White Throne judgement at the end of time!

Tim, Age 17
Florida

What will our glorified bodies look like?

Somewhat like the one you have now only perfect in every way (no one will be old). Your glorified body will be immortal, but you will be able to feel, hear, taste and see as you do now. It will never die, sin nor choose or desire anything but God's will.

Earlene, Age 58
Jacksonville, FL

Will we be able to sing in Heaven?

That is one thing that will bless everyone to know, we will all be able to sing. Even if you couldn't carry a note when you were on earth, in Heaven, you will sound glorious. Everyone worships God with their voice in Heaven.

Taylor, Age 10
Jacksonville, FL

Does Heaven ever change the way it looks over the years?

Yes, Heaven is always adding new things for us to do. Also, people are always going to Heaven, so mansions are continually being added. Eventually God will make a new earth and we will live there with God for eternity!

Antoinette, Age 16
Florida

What happens to unborn babies that died and are a result of sin?

When babies die they go to Heaven no matter how they were conceived. Life begins at conception, so whether miscarried or aborted; all babies go to Heaven. They will grow VERY slowly, but whatever 'gift' God gave them they will still get to use it in Heaven!

Trevor, Age 6
Florida

Are we going to die in Heaven?

No, but you have to die to go there. The bible says, "It is appointed unto man once to die". Once you die, your spiritual body (which lives inside your physical body) is taken up to Heaven, where you live a fantastic REAL life!

Brandon, Age 16
Florida

It is a common misconception, but do we really float on clouds in Heaven?

No. You do not float on clouds; you walk on heaven's ground. You can, however, float on the worship as it flows through the air and into the throne room. There is always spontaneous worship going on somewhere in Heaven and if you join in, you become a part of the worship and actually float with it.

Natalie, Age 35
Florida

I lost my best friend who was also a devoted wife and mother of a 7 year old. She passed away at age 31 leaving a grieving husband, son, and church. Why would God take her so seemingly early?

God does not take people early, He alone has numbered our days. We won't understand why some things happen until we stand before God, but we must trust Him in every situation. When someone goes to Heaven sooner than we expected, many times that's where their destiny will be completed. One thing you must know, God NEVER takes away our 'gifts', we will use them in Heaven to bless everyone!

Michael, Age 10
Jacksonville, FL

Would there be a new earth where nothing went wrong?

Yes, the Word says there will be a new Heaven and a new earth which will be perfect as the devil and all those who chose him will be in the Lake of Fire for eternity. Rev 21

Emily, Age 14
Jacksonville, FL

Are there oceans with sharks and jelly fish?

Yes, there is a crystal sea which comes from the river of life that flows out of God's throne. Also, the Bible states that there are fish of all kinds in the water and the crystal sea is big enough to hold huge sailing ships.

Steve, Age 11
Jacksonville, FL

What does God look like?

The bible says that Jesus is the 'express' image of the Father. That means an exact duplicate. So God looks like Jesus, except He is bigger. The light around God's face is so brilliant it is almost impossible to see that part of Him. He is a loving, Holy Father that can hardly wait to welcome us home to Heaven.

Kevin, Age 16
Florida

Is there a theme park?

I am delighted you asked! Yes, there is a fantastic amusement park, which I mention in the book. In that place, there is a huge roller coaster called "The Rush". There are some normal rides, but there are also supernatural rides that will blow you away. One of the amusements is to learn to fly like Superman!

Victoria, Age 17
Florida

Will we have any concept of time?

Not really, because you are in eternity and there is no time.
There are certain events that take place in Heaven and you are made
'aware' of the timing by the Spirit of God. He does this by speaking
directly to your spirit.

Klara, Age 5
Florida

If the bad guys turn good, can they go to Heaven?

Yes, God desires that <u>NONE</u> should perish. If anyone confesses
their sins, Jesus is faithful to cleanse and forgive them no matter
what they have done. I John 1:9

Caroline, Age 11
Jacksonville, FL

I would ask God how far Heaven is away from us.

God's home is a massive spiritual world bigger than our Galaxy
and exists in the Third Heaven. It is far above the earth's atmosphere, the universe and the Second heaven where satan has set up
his little counterfeit kingdom to rule over evil. We cannot see the
spirit realm with our physical eyes, but Heaven is supernatural and
is close enough to view our lives on earth.

Katrina, Age 41
Jacksonville, FL

Will I be around my family? (Kids, grandparents, spouse)

Yes, some really close knit families will live in areas I call "community dwellings" and the best way to describe what I saw was picturing a huge wagon wheel with many spokes and a center cap lying flat but no rim. The spokes would be the individual custom mansions for each family member and the "cap" in the center would represent the big common area to gather in. They also take turns staying in each other's mansions. No matter where we live in Heaven, it will be wonderful!

Christopher, Age 11
Jacksonville, FL

Could you watch the people on earth from Heaven?

Yes, you would go to the Portal which God made for just that purpose. They cheer you on from Heaven and still sing Happy Birthday to you! They also declare God's will for your life. Read Hebrews 12:1

Katie, Age 16
Florida

Will we remember our life on earth when we are in Heaven?

What God forgives, He remembers no more, but in Heaven, you retain all memories good or bad. You will not feel condemnation for any sins, because they were all forgiven. When we are living on the new earth that God has promised us, I believe all negative memories

139

will be removed. Everyone should live a Godly life by fleeing from sin and pursuing a personal relationship with Christ. This type of memory you create would always bless you.

Jessica, Age 10
Jacksonville, FL

Why do so many people die young and go to Heaven?

Perhaps their destiny was to be completed in Heaven and not on earth. God did not cause their death but knew the day they would come home to Heaven. They will still become what God purposed them to be as He still uses their gifts in Heaven!

Christie, Age 6
Florida

Do the tooth fairies live in Heaven?

No, but there are beautiful, small, delicate angels who take care of the waterfalls, streams and flowers.

Tyler, Age 17
Florida

Are there different levels of salvation?

No, you are either saved or not saved, but there are different levels of reward for your service to God and your kindness to mankind.

Katie, Age 5
Florida

God, can I live with you?

All those who accept Jesus as their savior will be living in Heaven with God. That is why He created us, so that He could have a family.

Neil, Age 17
Florida

Can we essentially get "kicked out" of Heaven for messing up once in Heaven?

You cannot mess up in Heaven, nor will God kick you out, because we will be perfect as Jesus is perfect. Once you get there, you will never be taken way from God.

Kyle, Age 10
Jacksonville, FL

Can we see things that we could not see before?

Yes, because we will be living in the spirit realm and we will be able to see spiritual things.

Gayle, Age 13
Jacksonville, FL

Do pets go to Heaven?

Yes, pets go to Heaven. I clearly saw several of our family pets in Heaven who are staying with my Father, including a Yorkie named Mr. Fuzz and Sally, an 1,100 pound pig. I also saw a duck named Max that was lovingly raised by my brother Joey. God created them as companions for us on earth and because He loves us so much, we get to continue that friendship with our pets forever. **Note: One third of all the 400 surveys asked this same question.**

Bryson, Age 17
Florida

As those who have answered the call unto salvation will be given bodies fashioned "unto his glorious body"
(Phi 3:21), will we be made in His physical likeness, or is such knowledge beyond mans comprehension?

We will not look like Christ, but like Him our bodies will no longer be mortal, which age and die, but we will be immortal forever.

Garrett, Age 11
Jacksonville, FL

Since everyone prayed to you, who did you pray to when you prayed?

God doesn't need to pray, because not only does He know the answers, He has the solution.

Kenny, Age 6
Jacksonville, FL

Will it (Heaven) ever be destroyed?

One day there will a new Heaven and a new earth. The old one will
be folded up like a garment. Read, Rev. 21

Erica, Age 10
Jacksonville, FL

**Doesn't Heaven ever get crowded, because every day some more
people go there?**

No, because Heaven is always expanding and Heaven is so big, they
have angels who live there that could hold our planet in their hand!

Brett, Age 17
Florida

**I've been told there will be mansions and streets of gold, but
shouldn't we not care about material possessions in Heaven?**

It is God's desire to bless His people, so these things and many more
are gifts for us to enjoy, their value is not viewed the same as they
were on earth..

Ashley, Age 10
Jacksonville, FL

Would there be a soccer field in Heaven?

Yes, they have many of the same sports as on earth and more because those are gifts God gave to them. The difference is sports are all played as a form of worship unto God. Each team has a place on the scoreboard, but all the points go to Jesus.

David, Age 16
Florida

Will there be a way for us to see those in Hell?

No, that would cause grief and pain, and neither of those exists in Heaven.

Cory, Age 17
Florida

Is there going to be a question for us to answer in order to get into Heaven and if so, what?

The only question I know of is, "Did you accept Jesus as your Savior and repent of your sins?"

Christina, Age 39
Callahan, FL

Will I recognize my children when we all get there?

Yes, you will recognize your children and family members. The bible says, "You will be known there as you were known on earth", except you will look a lot better!

Carlos, Age 6
Florida

How much does everything cost?

Nothing, it's all free!! Money is not necessary in Heaven because all things are given as gifts.

Trey, Age 10
Jacksonville, FL

Why is Heaven invisible?

We are "physical" beings and we see things with our physical eyes. However, Heaven exists in the spiritual realm, which is why it is invisible. When you die, your spirit body goes to Heaven and then everything is visible.

Kaitlyn, Age 12
Florida

Will we each have our own mansion or will there be a house for everyone to share?

God gives everyone their own mansion which is designed according to their gift; however many people do visit/stay with each other and even their family members. God knows what blesses you. There are also homes to use while visiting other areas of Heaven.

Nicholas, Age 11
Richmond, VA

What is Heaven like?

Heaven is similar to earth with many of the same things but it is perfect in every way. It is full of peace, joy, and fantastic things for us to do and have fun with. We will live in the awesome presence of God!

Lauren, Age 16
Florida

I know that when you get to Heaven, we supposedly will never be bored and will enjoy Heaven for all eternity. However, I can't stop thinking that Heaven will be boring and the concept of being somewhere forever scares me. Will we be bored in Heaven?

First of all, you will not be spending eternity in Heaven, but on the new earth. Remember, God does not give us a spirit of fear, but of love and a sound mind. Second, Heaven has so many radical fun things to do that there's no time to get bored. God is a creator and He is continually creating new things for us in Heaven, so no, you will never be bored!

Matthew, Age 17
Florida

Are there any wars against Hell in which all the people in Heaven and the angels fight? I want to slay a demon with a sword and shield.

There are several end time wars and battles mentioned in the book of Revelation and yes, the Redeemed living in Heaven will come back to earth with Jesus to fight in one of them!

Catherine, Age 12
Jacksonville, FL

Are we going to be clothed?

Yes, we have a gown of Salvation and a robe of Righteousness for corporate or united gatherings, but we will also have a wardrobe of many different tunic tops and pants, because there are so many things to do that you cannot do in a gown!

Will, Age 17
Florida

Why do you want me to come?

God loved you before you were born, because you came from Him. Christ came and died, so you can spend eternity with God. They wait every day, desiring that you will call out to them. If you were the only person on earth, Jesus would have died just for you, because He loves you that much. God has a purpose for your life now and in Heaven.

Trinity, Age 5
Richmond, VA

Will we have chocolate ice cream in Heaven?

Yes, because God gives us the desires of our hearts and because people have a 'gift' to create ice cream and you get to use your gifts in Heaven. I love chocolate ice cream too; also, because I was shown an ice cream parlor while I was visiting Heaven. The scoops were HUGE!!!

STANDING WITH ISRAEL –
GOD'S CHOSEN

My passion for Israel is not just something I believe in, it is a part of my heritage and was delighted the Father wanted to include this statement in the book.

The following was written, at the request of the Father, by Paul Wilbur of Paul Wilbur Ministries.

Should Christians stand with the modern state of Israel? Is there a real connection between the Jewish community of today and the ancient people of the Bible? Are the promises of God through the prophets and the Psalms of David still valid today? Didn't the Church take the place of Israel in God's plan when the Jews rejected Christ and handed Him over to the Romans to be crucified?

The problem as I see it, is not a matter of truthful answers, but rather a matter of historically bad teaching and bias that has masked the truth with traditions of men that have made the word of God "of no effect."

"How have we done this'" you might ask, "No one wants to be guilty of doing such a thing on purpose!" I am glad you asked, because it breaks ground for an honest look into the only answer we need, and they are contained within the pages of the Bible, God's word, perfect and eternal.

First of all, how we read the Bible, or better yet, how we understand the Bible is critical to our understanding of who the author is and what he has declared about Israel, covenant and the Jewish people. My dear friend John Bevere has been a Bible teacher for some twenty-five years, and on his last trip to Jacksonville he made a statement that will stick with me for the rest of my life! He said, and I paraphrase, "It is time for us to stop reading (the Bible) what we believe, and to start believing what we read!" Did you catch that? In other words, we are all guilty of reading the word of God through the rose colored glasses of the doctrines and traditions we have all been taught, rather than simply believing the words that we read on the page. We all feel inadequate at some point to completely and accurately understand and interpret certain passages of prophecy or allegory, so we turn to more learned men and women for help. The problem here is obvious; we each learn from one another, and sometimes we carry away 'truths' that are more tradition, conjecture or opinion than we were led to believe.

The sad thing to me as a Jewish believer is that so much of God's word could be so easily confused or misunderstood by more than 50% of the Church worldwide. All those promises that were made to Israel were contingent on how faithful she was as a nation? Wow, what a terrible standard and a burden-some stone to lay on anyone. How would you like all the promises of God to you to be contingent on how well the whole earth Church of America obeyed His commandments? No thank you!

So how should we understand the Bible on the subject of Israel and how should we respond to the Jewish people today? I have always believed that the Bible says what it means, and means what it says. Yes, there are many different kinds of Biblical language, prose, poetry, allegory, parables and the like, but most of it is pretty straightforward talk that is easily understood at face value. When God is speaking to Israel, He says so, and when He is speaking to the followers of Jesus, He makes it plain. It often takes several degrees and quite a few 'experts' to muddy it up beyond understanding!

So now that I have offended most of the educated world, or at least anyone with a few capital letters following their names, let's simply hear what the Bible has to say to and about Israel. When we know what the Creator of the Universe thinks about these things, it should make it a heck of a lot easier for us to make up our minds on which side of the debate we stand.

So let's hear from the author of the Bible, in His own words, what He thinks about Israel. (I have edited many of the following passages in order to conserve space without doing damage to the context. Any comments of mine will be in parenthesis.)

Is. 41:9-10 O Israel, I have chosen you and not rejected you... do not fear for I am your God...I will strengthen you and help you... ALL who rage against you will surely be ashamed and disgraced... those who oppose you will perish. (You do not need to hold a doctorate of history degree to know that every nation that opposed Israel was put to shame.)

Jer. 31:31 The time is coming, declares the Lord, when I will make a new covenant with the house of Israel and the house of Judah...For I will forgive their wickedness and will remember their sins no more...he who appoints the sun to shine by day, the moon and stars to shine by night, Adonai Sabbaoth is his name. Only if these decrees vanish from my sight will the descendants of Israel ever cease to be a nation before me.

Num. 23:19 God is not a man that he should lie, or the son of man that he should repent and change his mind. Has he spoken and not performed it, or has he promised and not made it good?

Roms. 11:1-22 I ask then, did God reject his people? BY NO MEANS! I am talking to you Gentiles... for if Israel's rejection is the reconciliation of the nations, what will Israel's acceptance be but life from the dead...(resurrection, the return of Yeshua, the Kingdom on earth). If the firstfruits is holy then the whole batch is holy; if the root is holy, so are the branches. Do not be arrogant, but be afraid. For if God did not spare the natural branches, he will not spare you either! (These are tough words, but the wise will humble themselves and take heed to what the Spirit of God is saying, even to the Church!)

Is. 49:22-23 Behold I will lift up my hand in an oath to the nations, and they shall bring your sons in their arms, and your daughters shall be carried on their shoulders. Kings shall be your fathers and queens your nursing mothers; they shall bow before you with their faces to the earth and lick the dust of your feet. Then you will know that I am the Lord.

Joel 2:23-26 Be glad then you children of Zion, and rejoice in the Lord your God; and he will cause the rain to come down for you-the former rain and the latter rain...the threshing floors shall be full of wheat, and the vats shall overflow with new wine and oil. So I will restore to you the years that the locust has eaten...you shall eat and be satisfied, and praise the Name of the Lord your God; and my people Israel shall never be put to shame.

Obviously, these are just a small sampling of the hundreds of promises the God of Abraham, Isaac and Jacob has made to his people Israel. Isn't it just a little obvious to the casual observer when he uses the names of patriarchs of Israel for his own name?! He is identified many times in the scriptures in this way and never seems to mind. Even the life of Jesus parallels the life of Israel in many startling and amazing ways; born in Israel, went to Egypt, death of the innocents, and many more examples

Should Christians stand with Israel? I like to answer that question rather simply; does God love Israel?...then so should you!

ABOUT THE AUTHOR

I accepted Jesus at age 4 and have had a close relationship with Him ever since. I have not led a perfect life, but quickly repented when I would sin. My Dad set a wonderful example for me and since I worked closely with him in his ministry of helping people for over 18 years, my life has become an extension of his! I talk about my family a lot, because while growing up, they were all I had. Each of my sisters and brothers had special gifts and talents that are used by God to bless people. They helped me to become who I am and I will always love them. 'Things' were not that important in our home and although we did not have much, we shared what we had. God will always use people who are willing to get out of their comfort zones and do something to help others.

If you are interested in my 'religious' credentials, here they are: I am a licensed minister (since 1981) although I do not use the title and have operated in the prophetic (with a 'seer' anointing, which is given only by God) for over 25 years, and ministered with several prophetic teams. Through my home church, New Life Christian Fellowship, I was a member of our 'citywide' intercessory group, a member of the 'altar' ministry team, served in children's church, vacation bible school and headed up the pastor's hospitality team. Volunteered for many positions at numerous conferences for various ministries and have been a part of our families' Victory ministry team for over 20 years.

The credentials which most impress the Lord are as follows: Honoring my parents at all times, not just as a child, but even now as an adult. Also submitting to my wonderful husband (as my cover, protector & my love) for over 29 years; even when I did not understand his decisions. Always teaching the things of God to my three daughters by LIVING the Word and not just speaking it! We gave extravagantly, even after losing everything during a season of our life and having to sleep on someone else's floor. Developed a lifestyle of Abandoned Worship regardless of circumstances or situations evident in our lives; trusting Him like a child, unquestionably! Being thankful for everything He gives us, even the small things! Sharing what I have with others when they are in need. Setting aside hours every evening to worship and pray; and then waking every morning to greet The Father, my Lord Jesus and my best friend, Holy Spirit. A life lived for them and helping others are my greatest credentials!

One way you can begin to develop a relationship with the Lord is get in a room by yourself to play anointed worship music and just sit and 'soak' as God inhabits the praises of His people even on CDs. You will feel His presence and then start telling Him how much you want to know Him (don't give a list of your needs at this time), let Him know how grateful you are for His sacrifice. Start with just 10 minutes and slowly increase the time you give to Him. You will begin to feel differently as His love and life begins to fill you!

I am so honored that God chose me for this assignment, even though I never asked for it. Because I had made a covenant with Him to use me in any manner He desired, it was His decision to take me to Heaven. You must live a 'surrendered' life to the will of the Father if you wish to pursue this type of intimate relationship.

Prior to my experiences in Heaven, I had worked for twenty four years in key positions in the business world and now I am the President of One Quest International Corp. which was founded for the purpose of revealing Heaven to the earth through the Marketplace and providing 'Kingdom' finances. Many projects are planned to take place in the near future to fulfill that vision.

I love HIM
I love HIS Word
I love His presence
I love His sacrifice

I love His Father
I love His home, Heaven and
I love His people (that would be you)

I do realize not everyone will accept or even want the revelations in this book and I FORGIVE anyone, in advance, for wrongly accusing me, lying about me or cursing me. The enemy will try everything he can to stop me, but IT IS TOO LATE, I have died to myself and found my life in CHRIST!

STATEMENT OF FAITH

I believe in and know that EL, I AM, is the one true God. He is the Creator of all things and holds the air we breathe in His hand! I believe and know that He has always existed and always will. He did not just appear somewhere in eternity; eternity exists in Him.

I believe and know that this living God (who is a member of the Trinity) 'spoke' and the Word, who was with Him, created mankind in the Garden of Eden, which in the beginning was perfect and without sin. Then he (satan) who birthed iniquity, tempted Adam & Eve and by their choice to believe the enemy and through disobedience, lost their relationship with God and gave away their dominion.

I believe and know that God made a way back to Himself through the offering of His only Son, Jesus, (who was the Word made flesh) born through immaculate conception and then crucified on the cross at Calvary to pay the price to free us from sin. By acceptance of this blood sacrifice, man is counted as righteous, his dominion restored and is given eternal life.

I believe and know that we, as Believers, are made in their (the Trinity) image and after their likeness and have been given dominion and authority over the whole earth. Also, that we have power over ALL the power of the enemy (satan).

I believe and know that as Believers, we have access to and can invite, the third member of the Trinity, Holy Spirit to 'in-dwell' and 'fill us' with a layer of His being (which is a whole of Him) and then we become the temple of the Holy Spirit! One of the outward signs (evidence) of this is speaking in unknown tongues, which is not understood by our natural minds, nor is it understood by the enemy! It is also a way to build up oneself in your most holy faith!

I believe and know that the Holy Bible is the Word of God, inspired and ordered by Him. It brings life, edification, correction and knowledge of the One who made us and His house called Heaven. It is an instruction book on how to stay free from sin, create a habitation for Heaven in our homes and live a victorious life so that our souls may prosper and bring Glory to God.

I believe and know of and have been shown the powerful days of Greater Glory that are about to rock and stun this world with the passion, power and purposes of God! For a long season on this earth, we will Manifest as the Sons and Daughters of the Most High God and help erase the 'lie' that says there is no God! This is the time the Father calls the Kingdom Age! Darkness will be pushed back and there shall be Regions of Light established where crime and evil will flee as we lay down our lives, die to self and allow God to direct our paths. God is about to pour out His Spirit (with Baptism in Fire) and touch all flesh (without their permission)! The Kingdom of God will be clearly seen by this world through the Body of Christ allowing His will to be done on earth as it is in Heaven. These things will take place before the perilous times and before the Tribulation. Wake up, unpack your suitcase and get ready to run your race with the Host of Heaven!!

CONTACT INFORMATION

Kat has **MANY** other products (DVDs, CDs, Audio Books) that contain revelations not mentioned in any of the books. We also offer colored copies of all the illustrations found in the books. For a full products catalog to be sent via email or regular mail, call our office.

PHONE NUMBER FOR ORDERING PRODUCTS:

904-527-1943

Or visit our WEBSITE: www.revealingheaven.com

To contact us concerning things other than orders, please **EMAIL** us at contactoqi@revealingheaven.com or use our

MAILING ADRESS:
One Quest International Corp
P. O. Box 550989
Jacksonville, FL 32255

IF YOU ARE INTERESTED IN BOOKING KAT TO SPEAK,

Please visit our website for further instructions.

PLEASE NOTE: It is not possible to contact Kat personally to speak to her, to answer prayer requests or to answer emails due to her extremely busy schedule. She cares very deeply about each person and will make every effort to reveal Heaven through her messages and website content. Her commission is to see Heaven and Share, she does not do individual ministry of any kind as the Lord said she was to deliver a message to the CORPORATE Body of Christ. Thank you for respecting what God has asked of her life! Bless you all!

We are not a ministry, but a business with Heart and a President who does outreach ministry. We do not have on staff intercessors who pray for callers, but there are many other groups and ministries who will be glad to help you in this area of need.

If you desire to bless Kat with a love offering to help take this message to the world, you may visit Katkerr.com and go to the Treasury to give, or, if you prefer you may make checks payable to Kat Kerr and mail to P. O. Box 551513, Jacksonville, FL 32255. While she cannot give you a tax deductible receipt, we are certain that God will reward you abundantly because you will be helping her to reveal Heaven to earth and we know Kat will be very grateful!

NOTES

PRAYER LIST